She Called Him Raymond

A True Story Of Love, Loss,
Faith And Healing

Praise for Ray O'Conor's
She Called Him Raymond
A True Story Of Love, Loss, Faith And Healing

"Ray O'Conor abandoned his career to search for his namesake, a heroic B-17 pilot who died in World War II. What he found touches the heart and stirs the soul."
James Bradley
#1 New York Times Best Selling Author of *Flags of Our Fathers* and *The China Mirage.*

"A remarkable story of family, loyalty and heroism. O'Conor's narrative inspires while tearing a hole in your heart."
Brig. Gen. William Martin, U.S. Army, Ret.

"Beautifully written and extraordinarily moving. I couldn't put it down."
Teri P. Gay
Historian and Author of *Strength Without Compromise*

"This gripping narrative that lives in a son's heart, is a story that had to be told."
Winifred Yu
Journalist and Author

"A poignant and thrilling American story, told with sensitivity and grace."
Congressman Chris Gibson
Veteran, Operations Desert Storm and Iraqi Freedom
Colonel, U.S. Army, Ret.

"A heroic tale of love, life, family, country and devotion. A compellingly written story about people we all knew, or thought we did."
Congressman Bill Owens, Ret.
Former Captain, U.S. Air Force

SHIRES PRESS
4869 Main Street
P.O. Box 2200
Manchester Center, VT 05255
www.northshire.com

She Called Him Raymond
A True Story Of Love, Loss, Faith And Healing
Copyright © 2015 by Ray O'Conor
www.shecalledhimraymond.com

ISBN Number: 978-1-60571-271-0

Cover Design & Interior Designed by: Debbi Wraga

First Paperback Edition

Printed in the United States of America

For a lovely couple!

Warmest regards,

Ray O'C

She Called Him Raymond

A True Story Of Love, Loss, Faith And Healing

Ray O'Conor

Dedication

I owe a deep debt of gratitude to Helen and
Raymond that I will never be able to repay. This story
began to unfold for them during the Summer of 1942,
and for me, sixty-three years later.

Table of Contents

About This Book

This is a narrative non-fiction book. The story is true. The characters are real. During the years that I researched and wrote this book, I found and interviewed all of the individuals who played a significant role who I believed to still be alive. Multiple personal interviews, extensive conversations, and exchanges of letters and emails were critical to the successful completion of this project. In the recreation of scenes, the dialogue was recounted to me in an interview, quoted from records or letters, or deduced from inquiry and investigation.

Hundreds of letters, personal journals, and family records were examined. A myriad of photographs were discovered and collected. Countless hours were spent finding and reviewing military personnel records, combat reports, government documents and other evidence to properly and accurately portray the people, places, and events presented here.

This story moves back and forth over decades. Most of the women and men in this story died before the book was completed. I pray that as I narrate this story on their behalf, I do so effectively, thoroughly, and with the respect and dignity they deserve.

A letter penned in 1944 uncovers the powerful and heartfelt story of Helen Gregg, the daughter of Irish immigrant parents who grew up in the miseries of Hell's Kitchen during the Great Depression, and Clarence Raymond Stephenson, a young aspiring B-17 pilot raised in the small, struggling city of Ironton, Ohio. Fate brings them together in New York's Central Park in 1942. From the moment their eyes first met, they knew their lives would never be the same.

This captivating and poignant story of their struggles and romance, his exploits as a highly decorated B-17 pilot during World War II, and the tragedy that tears them apart, will inspire you while tugging at your heart.

With sensitivity and grace, Ray O'Conor reveals a secret about the dashing and brave young aviator who stole Helen's heart, and he divulges a promise that Helen made to Raymond in the summer of 1942 that she had to keep, no matter how long or how hard it might be to fulfill.

Theirs is a compelling story of two ordinary people who led extraordinary lives during the most tumultuous period in history.

1940's • 1950's • 1960's • 1970's • 1980's • 1990's • 2000's • 2010's

SEPTEMBER 6, 2005

A Birthday Surprise

Her head is full of thoughts
she was sure would have faded by now.
— *Anonymous*

My mom, Helen, was never much for being made a fuss over, but she would have to tolerate a bit of it today. I sat behind the steering wheel of my car for the three and a half hour drive south from Saratoga Springs in upstate New York, to the village of Floral Park on Long Island. I thought of the life our family had shared. It all seemed commonplace, even a little boring. A mom and a dad, daughter and three sons, growing up in middle class America, just like millions of others.

Mom and Dad moved to their small, modest cape-style home about forty years earlier. A simple, two-story, white stucco house with three small bedrooms that my folks, two brothers, sister, and I shared. Mom planted rose bushes along the side yard of the house that yielded beautiful red, pink, and white roses every year. The porch on the front of the house was where our family spent a considerable amount of time sitting, talking, or watching the neighbors and cars pass by along Beverly Avenue.

We played cards on many evenings: rummy, hearts, and a game called "Knucks." The object of the game was to dispose of your cards as quickly as possible. The last player holding any cards received a rap on the knuckles from each player with the deck for every card he or she held. Mom played Knucks as a kid on the streets of New York City. Time stood still as we played cards, talked, joked, and shouted hellos to the neighbors who passed by. We enjoyed being a family.

A basketball hoop hung from the front of the garage that my brothers, our friends, and I played hoops on as kids. The garage door served as a backstop for playing Whiffle ball or stickball. The concrete driveway was our basketball court and baseball field.

Just about every house on the street was similar. For the most part the outside of my folks' house looked the same as when they bought it. Not much had changed on the inside either. Most of the furnishings that were moved into our house originally, were still contained within. Mom wasn't much for changes. She was committed to getting the most out of the useful life of anything that was purchased or passed down from others in the family.

In the 1950s and '60s when I was a little boy and we lived in the Jackson Heights neighborhood in the Borough of Queens, our favorite store for clothing and household furnishings was a place Mom called Sally's. I thought it was the same as any other department store, but Sally's was a pseudonym for the Salvation Army thrift store.

Mom never spoke much about her past, but on this day, her eightieth birthday, September 6, 2005, she shared a few stories about when she grew up in New York City during the Great Depression. She never complained about the circumstances of her upbringing, which to me seemed pretty dire. She was usually happy and always content. I think she wanted me and my siblings to understand how fortunate we were to have avoided that era and to be thankful for all that we had – a roof over our heads, shoes under our feet, food in our bellies, and, most importantly, our health and each other.

She hoped someday her grandchildren and great-grandchildren would understand as well, and appreciate the modest roots of our family. To realize that hard work and patience might fulfill the dream of a good life. She regularly instructed my older sister Ann Marie, big brother Joe, younger brother Marty, and me about the virtues of thrift. She used phrases such as, *It's not how much you make it's how much you spend that counts.* And Benjamin Franklin's adage, *Neither a lender nor borrower be,* to make her point. Mom's parents and her brothers and sisters never had much money, or much of anything for that matter, but she said they were always rich in family.

About mid-afternoon, Mom quietly asked me if I could help her with something in her bedroom. She was pretty handy around the house, but as she aged she asked me to do a bit of home repair or take on a task to spruce up the house when I came to visit. She told me once that she was very disappointed as a school girl that only boys were allowed to take wood working and other trade classes in school. She always preferred to do for herself, regardless of whether it was typically a boy or girl chore that needed doing. Mom always found something that needed doing.

Once inside her bedroom, she closed the door and began rummaging through the bottom of a dresser drawer. As Mom searched, I gazed around her bedroom noticing that in addition to being seriously outdated, the seams of the 70's era floral print wallpaper were coming undone in a few spots. I hoped that its removal and replacement was not

what needed doing that day. Mom eventually unearthed an old and scuffed wooden box. In that box appeared to be some keepsakes including a set of wooden rosary beads, a few photographs and an old prayer book. I also saw an envelope in the box that she ever so gently removed.

"Here it is. This is what I need your help with," she said.

She patted her hand on the edge of the bed, "Sit down here."

We both sat down on the edge of the bed next to each other. The envelope she held in her hand was clearly weathered by age as many years of oxidation rendered the paper yellow and fragile. Although always vibrant, active, and strong, Mom was showing some signs of fragility too. Her hands trembled and there was a perceptible shortness of breath from having made the effort to extract the wooden box from the depths of the lowest dresser drawer. Her full head of hair was still thick and wavy as it was in her younger days, but what were just a few silver streaks through her hair not all that long ago, had now crowded out her once dark mane.

"There's a letter in this envelope," she said. "Would you please read it to me?"

Mom's vision had deteriorated over the years due to macular degeneration. Even while wearing her glasses, or in concert with a magnifying glass, she was no longer able to read the small print written on the pages she held. She seemed nervous and quite anxious as she handed the letter to me. Her hands now shook markedly and her breaths quickened.

Given the fragile nature of the letter, I delicately removed it from the envelope. The return address on the envelope read C.R. Stephenson 1st LTAC. The name wasn't familiar to me. The post mark date was September 6, 1944. It was mailed on the day Mom celebrated her nineteenth birthday.

"Please, Raymond, go ahead and read it to me," Mom said in a faint voice.

As I began to read the letter, Mom placed my left hand between both of hers.

I uttered the salutation, "My Dearest Darling." After saying just those few words, I could see tears well up in my mother's eyes.

"Are you okay, Mom?"

"Yes, please keep reading," she uttered as her voice cracked.

"But what's this all about, Mom?"

"Keep going, Raymond. I'll explain later."

As I continued to read each word aloud, Mom became more overwhelmed with emotion. She squeezed my hand as I read each passage to her. Sixty-one years had passed since that letter was written and my mother first read it. Sitting there, watching her reaction to hearing those words, it was as though she was listening to them for the first time. I was unaware of what it all meant or what happened in 1944 that this letter could evoke such an emotional response from her more than six decades later.

I finished reading the letter to her, tears trickling down her cheeks.

"There's something I've wanted to tell you for a long time. I wanted to tell you many times before, but there are some things that I thought should be left in the past. Some things just shouldn't be talked about after so much time has gone by. And besides, I worried that if your father knew, it would upset him. But, who knows how long I have on this earth? I've waited long enough to share this story with you. But, you have to promise me that this will stay just between you and me."

"But why, Mom?"

"If your father knew, it would hurt his feelings. You know I'd never say anything to hurt your father. You'll understand better when I'm done. So, you promise?"

"Okay, Mom. I promise. Not a word to anyone."

1880's • 1890's • 1900's • 1910's • 1920's • 1930's • 1940's • 1950's

↑

1942

Sister, Can You Spare A Nickel?

I have two feet to walk and two hands to hold.
I have two ears to hear and two eyes to see.
I have only one heart though.
The other was given to another, who I have not yet found.

— Anonymous

Helen Gregg and two friends, Jean and Joan, sisters with whom Helen worked, decided to spend the afternoon of June 13, 1942 in New York City's Central Park. The park offered some relief from the heat as the cool grass, the shade of the trees, and the tranquil waters of Central Park Lake were a stark contrast to the sweltering temperatures that day in the Gregg family apartment and along the concrete sidewalks and blacktopped streets that radiated the summer's heat. Not only was it a break from the heat, but an escape from the tenements and squalor of their neighborhood.

Late in the afternoon, the three young ladies decided to make their way back home. They approached the southern edge of the park near 59th Street, hurrying to get home in time for supper. Meals were never a certainty, so they seldom chanced missing one. The girls were so engaged in their conversation as they rushed through the park, they barreled into a soldier and two sailors in uniform.

After the initial surprise of the collision, the three young ladies and men looked up at each other and laughed. Although not necessarily their fault, the sailors and soldier apologized. Helen was immediately drawn to the young soldier. She couldn't say with absolute certainty whether it was his boyishly handsome face, piercing blue eyes, warm smile or sculpted six-foot frame that attracted her to him. She never had a feeling quite like this about any of the boys in her neighborhood, or the fellows with whom she attended school or met at work.

He was immediately taken with her too. Helen was pretty with thick, wavy dark hair and intense hazel eyes. She had soft features and wore no makeup. Her skin was flawless. The late afternoon sun glowing behind her created a halo around her dark hair. He looked beyond her simple, second hand, off the rack from Sally's, white blouse and blue skirt. He saw a vivacious and lively young lady. Still more boy at heart than a man, he stood there in his Army Air Corps Cadet uniform as though ordered to attention. He was practically nose to nose with Helen as his pulse galloped. Something came over him. Was this an infatuation? What some folks call love at first sight? He couldn't say, not knowing. He had never been in love. He detected a certain spunkiness about her that he found captivating. He never had such a strong attraction toward any of the girls he knew back home in Ironton, or any place else he had been for that matter.

Although Jean and Joan thought the sailors were cute, Helen was wary of them. She was never one to prejudge, but her mother told her to stay away from sailors. They were nothing but trouble according to Maggie Gregg. Helen assumed her mother's reservations concerning sailors were driven by the horrible experiences her eldest daughter Mary had with her first husband, a sailor, who abused her. Although she questioned her mother's judgment, Helen knew it was best never to bring a sailor home to meet Mom.

"I am so sorry," the young soldier said to Helen. "Are you alright?"

Helen looked at the name tag that hung from his uniform. *Clarence R. Stephenson.*

"Clarence," she said in a somewhat disappointed tone.

"Yes," he said defensively. "Clarence is my name and it just happens to be my father's name as well."

"What does the R stand for on your name tag?"

"The R is for Raymond."

"I like that name. So, I will call you Raymond."

Raymond smiled. "Some of my friends back home in Ohio call me Raymond. That way folks don't confuse me with my dad. You can call me Raymond if it pleases you."

"It does and I will."

"And what about your name?" Raymond inquired.

"I'm Helen. Helen Gregg."

The two of them chatted for a bit about where they were from and why Raymond was in New York City. He told Helen that he was there to attend the Air Corp Technical Training School and was being housed at Mitchell Field on Long Island.

"I'm on my way to Penn Station on 33rd Street to catch a train back to my barracks."

"I live on 47th Street and am on my way home for supper."

"Can I walk you home, Helen?"

"If it pleases you, Raymond."

"It does and I will."

Jean, Joan, and the sailors were headed in the same direction, so the six of them headed south on 7th Avenue. As they strolled along and talked, no longer in so much of a hurry, Raymond reached into his pants pockets and realized he did not have enough money to afford the train fare back to Mitchell Field.

"Uh oh. Shoot."

"What's the matter, Raymond?"

"I don't have enough money for the train fare back to base."

"How much more do you need?"

"I'm a nickel short."

"Let me check my purse. I might have a nickel."

Overhearing this conversation, Jean and Joan, who were among New York City's poorest victims of the depression, who had even lived in a car for a time, interjected.

"I see what's going on here," Joan said.

"Yeah, Helen," Jean interrupted. "You're getting sweet talked out of a nickel. Tell that jerk to get lost. Go mooch your nickel off someone else, buddy."

Helen had an affinity for soldiers, especially since some of her brothers had enlisted in the army. She liked Raymond,

Helen's 47th Street tenement building (Building with ground floor arched windows and door).

thought him sincere and trusted him. Without hesitation, she gladly gave him her last nickel for his train fare.

Helen and Raymond continued to walk and chat while the two sailors and girls jabbered along. After reaching Helen's building on 47th Street, just west of 9th Avenue, she and Raymond bid their companions goodbye and then sat on the brown-stone front stoop for a while to get to know each other better. Helen felt a special connection between the two of them. Raymond felt that way too. There probably weren't two places in the country more different than New York City's West Side and Ironton, Ohio, but there was clearly something they shared.

Helen and Raymond had a certain innocence and naiveté about them. Neither had ever been in a serious romantic relationship. Raymond's assignment to New York for training took him outside of Ohio for the first time. Helen had never traveled beyond New York City. She envisioned Ohio as being all farm land with little civilization to speak of.

Raymond marveled at the commotion and bustle of New York. Its towering buildings, throngs of pedestrians, the traffic, the subway system, and all of its attractions and landmarks fascinated him. He was warned by his parents to be wary of city people, but for the most part, folks in New York City treated him kindly and, in particular, he found young Miss Gregg to be especially friendly and delightful. He never figured that he might fall for a city girl. What would his mom and dad think of him being sweet on a girl from New York City?

As the afternoon sun began to settle behind the tall buildings and cast a shadow along 47th Street, a loud voice bellowed from the fifth floor fire escape above. In an Irish brogue so thick you could cut it with a knife, Maggie Gregg called down to her daughter on the steps below, "Time for supper, Helen!"

"I'll be right up, Mom," Helen shouted toward the sky from the front stoop. "Raymond, I'm sorry, but I have to go."

She knew the risks of falling for a soldier. She already worried about her brothers who enlisted. Helen saw the broken bodies of boys coming home from the war. At Holy Mass every Sunday, Father Mulligan implored the faithful at

Sacred Heart Church to pray for the wounded, the missing, and the dead. Funeral processions heading to and from all of the neighborhood churches with flag covered coffins, followed by mourning family and friends, were a reminder of the perils of every man in uniform.

"I would like to see you again, Raymond."

"I would love to see you again too, Helen. I want to learn everything about you, but we've had so little time today."

Raymond wanted to give Helen a kiss before they parted, even if it was just on the cheek. He decided though, it would not be appropriate for a young gentleman who was brought up proper. So, they simply agreed on a subsequent day and time to meet again and bid each other good night.

When Raymond left Patterson Field in Dayton, Ohio for New York City, his entire focus was on fulfilling his goal of becoming a pilot in the Army Air Corps. He had no intention or desire to be distracted from that objective and he certainly didn't plan to become infatuated with a girl from New York City.

Helen thought this might be the start of something special. Her mother often told her that some of the most common occurrences of the day might be "signs" or special messages from God about things to come. Perhaps her chance meeting with a young man from Ohio in Central Park was just such a sign. Helen believed that happily ever after only occurred in fairy tales. It never seemed to happen to anyone in her neighborhood. But maybe, just maybe, happy endings really did exist.

After he rode the train from Manhattan back to his barracks, Raymond reached into his footlocker and pulled out his small, leather-bound diary. He hopped onto his bunk, unlocked the diary's small brass latch and excitedly wrote,

JUNE 13

1942. Met a lovely girl in Central Park and liked her very much. I made a date with her for next Thursday. Miss Helen Bragg. 424 W. 47th St. I feel this will change my entire future life.

Raymond tucked his diary away back in his footlocker. He stretched out and settled into his bunk for the night. He tossed and turned for hours. He couldn't get Helen's image out of his mind. Was he crazy about her, or just plain crazy? Questions raced through his mind. How old is she? Where are her people from? Is she a Christian? What did he actually know about her? Not much, really. But in his heart, he knew that the moment his eyes met hers, their lives would never be the same.

1880's • 1890's • 1900's • 1910's • 1920's • 1930's • 1940's • 1950's
↑
1912-1938

From County Longford to Ellis Island

In each family a story is playing itself out,
and each family's story embodies its hope and despair.
—Auguste Napier

Like many others of that era, Helen's mother, Margaret "Maggie" McGrath Gregg, came to this country with her husband, Martin Gregg, through Ellis Island in New York Harbor from Ireland. They arrived on April 25, 1923 with little more than the clothes they wore. Maggie was pregnant with her first child. She was a hearty woman who worked since childhood on a farm and in the family owned McGrath's Pub in the small village of Ballinalee in County Longford. She married Martin in 1923 at the age of twenty-nine. Many an unmarried

Maggie in the doorway of the McGrath family home and pub in the late 1800s, Ballinalee, Ireland.

woman at that age was thought to be a spinster or old maid and considered a burden on the family. She was fortunate to have finally married, but as her life with Martin unfolded, she thought otherwise.

Maggie was a fair skinned woman with bright hazel eyes and long, thick, dark brown hair. She was a woman not only powerful in physical stature, but equally strong in her Roman Catholic faith. Whether her children were heading out to school in the morning, or the ice man was leaving the apartment after dropping off a block of ice for the ice box, "God be with you. God bless you. God save you," was ritually spoken to all when leaving her company. No Sunday or holy day of obligation passed without Maggie attending Mass. The occasion of Ash Wednesday was always apparent by the black cinders that adorned her forehead. The image of the Sacred Heart of Jesus was ever present on her bedroom wall. A small statue of the Blessed Virgin Mary graced the top of the nightstand beside her bed. She knelt by the side of her bed every evening to recite the Holy Rosary before going to sleep.

When Maggie met her husband, he was a widower. Martin was five years Maggie's senior. He originally came to the United States of America with his first wife, Mary, in 1912 and became a naturalized citizen five years later. Martin was a farmer in Ireland as was his father, but times were hard there. Martin was poor and thin as a rail. Like millions of others who passed through Ellis Island from all over the world, he was looking for a new opportunity and a brighter future in America. During the first five years of marriage with Mary, she gave birth to four children, two boys and two girls. The first of the children to arrive was little Mary in 1913, next was Peter, born a year later, followed closely by Katherine and Martin, Jr.

The fruitful Mary Gregg informed her prodigiously potent husband that she was pregnant yet again in 1920. At some point during that pregnancy, Mary Gregg died. No one is certain how or why. Some in the family believed it was a complication related to her pregnancy. Others suspected Mary had an abortion. She was thirty three years old and had given birth to four children over the past five years. She and Martin were distraught over financial problems and struggling to feed themselves, plus the four children they were already raising. Being illegal, abortions were often back alley jobs that on occasion were fatal not only for the fetus, but the mother as well. Some in the family believed Martin forced his wife to have an abortion. Others claim that it was Mary who pursued that course and Martin didn't even know about it.

Martin "Pop" Gregg and his daughter, Mary, 1913.

After Mary's death, Martin couldn't find a suitable new wife in New York City. He decided to return to Ireland to find a new bride and a mother for his four children. It was too difficult for him to travel back to Ireland with all four of his offspring, so he took only his oldest son, Peter, back to Ireland with him. Mary, Katherine, and Martin, ages eight, four, and three respectively, were left at an orphanage in New York

Maggie McGrath Gregg and her son, William, 1924.

City. A tearful Martin pledged to the good Sisters of Charity and to his children that he would return for them some day. Brokenhearted without a mother and feeling abandoned by their father, Mary, Katherine, and Martin kissed "Pop" goodbye. He left America for Ireland on May 5, 1922.

Martin made good on his pledge. Nearly one year later, he traveled back to New York from Ireland. He returned with Maggie, his new wife, but without his eldest son Peter whom he allowed to stay in Ireland with relatives. Peter wasn't much for school and wanted to stay in Ireland where school attendance was not mandatory. Martin rationalized that Peter's mouth would be one less to feed for now.

Maggie and Martin added four more children to the family. William, Helen, Joseph, and John in that order. They, along with Martin's children from his previous marriage, rounded out a family of nine. They all became genuinely close, both emotionally and physically. Two adults and seven children were all housed in small apartments, in a series of very impoverished neighborhoods on Manhattan's West Side. For a time, Martin's younger sister, Annie Gregg, also lived with them. She worked as a chamber maid and helped the family financially by sharing a portion of her sparse earnings.

Of the two apartments where the family spent most of their lives together, the first was on West 36th Street between 9th Avenue and 10th Avenue. Their apartment was on the bottom floor of a five-story tenement building. Martin was fortunate, given the economic despair of the times, his lack of formal education, and his Irish heritage, to secure a job as the building's janitor. The wages he earned, although meager, were enough to keep the family fed. The rent charged on the apartment was discounted. It made raising a large family manageable. The apartment had four small rooms including a kitchen with a black coal stove and ice box, a living room, and one long bedroom. There was no electricity or central heat in the apartment. Gas lamps hung on the walls for light. The kitchen's coal stove served the dual purpose of a cooking and heating appliance. Given the condition of the building, with wall mounted gas lamps and the fire in the coal stove for heating and cooking, it was a miracle the whole building and the rest of the neighborhood never burned to the ground.

The children slept two or three to a bed in the cold water flat. A tattered curtain hung from the ceiling separating the sleeping quarters between the parents and their children. No one complained during the winter about having to share a bed, as having bunkmates made sleeping conditions warmer. The summers were another story though. At times the days and nights were sweltering hot, with no respite from the heat.

Families like the Greggs were desperately and unsuccessfully trying to recover from the 1929 stock market crash and subsequent economic collapse. Businesses in the cities were laying off workers and many of them shut down, putting millions of people out of work. More than a thousand banks went out of business and many individuals lost their investments and savings whether in the stock market or in a bank account.

Although there was a sink in the Gregg's tiny apartment kitchen, modern plumbing was lacking. A shared bathroom was located down the hall and a periodic bath or shower meant a trip to the neighborhood bath house a block or so away. Many people were fearful in the 1930s of losing what they had. Loss of money and loss of possessions was painful. The Gregg children had little fear though. They had so little to lose. As Spartan as their existence was and in spite of the harsh economic conditions, they had faith, they had each other and with that, they had enough.

About the mid 1930s, Maggie and her children noticed peculiar and sometimes dramatic changes in the behavior of their husband and father. Martin began experiencing periods of great anxiety and displayed moods that would swing like a pendulum from joy to despair. As time went on, his behavior became increasingly odd. He was fired from his job as the janitor of their apartment building. His dismissal meant the family would be put out on the street the next day. With what little savings they had, they were fortunate to secure an apartment on West 47th Street between 9th and 10th Avenues.

Pop, as Helen and her brothers and sisters called their father, never acted extremely crazy or dangerous. He spent hours just staring out a window or pacing slowly back and forth from one end of the apartment to the other muttering to himself. The way he mumbled, he couldn't be understood most of the time.

The Gregg's new apartment was on the top floor, the fifth, of a brownstone tenement. For the first time they had a working toilet in their apartment. Baths and showers still required a walk to the neighborhood bath houses. Electricity was an added luxury that came with the move, but a coal burning stove still provided heat and a cooking surface. The Greggs couldn't afford an electric refrigerator, so they dragged their ice box from the old apartment to 47th Street.

There were some early protests from the children about the effort required to climb all of the flights of stairs to reach their new dwelling on the top floor. Their mother admonished them in her Irish brogue.

"Quit 'yer gripin' and belly achin' and just give thanks be to God that 'yer lucky to have a roof over 'yer head!"

1880's • 1890's • 1900's • 1910's • 1920's • 1930's • 1940's • 1950's
↑
1930's

Brother, Can You Spare A Dime?

They used to tell me I was building a dream,
With peace and glory ahead,
Why should I be standing in line,
Just waiting for bread?

—*Yip Harburg*

New York City was a place of desperate poverty during The Great Depression, but you'd have never known it by observing Helen Gregg. She didn't understand how poor she was; because no one in the neighborhood was any better off. Steady work and regular meals were not always available, but the family managed to get by. No one locked their doors. You knew and trusted your neighbors and besides, most folks didn't have anything worth stealing. If a neighbor was desperate, you shared what you had or what you could afford with each other.

Born on September 6, 1925, Helen spent most of her young life on the top floor of the tenement building on 47th Street. Daily life was tempered by the harsh economic realities of the 1930s and 40s and the overshadowing of World War II. A slice of toast and a cup of water, milk, or coffee constituted a typical breakfast for Helen each day. It was the most important meal of the day. Some days it was the only meal. A hamburger and a potato were more than adequate for supper. A midday meal was optional dictated by whether or not there was enough food to go around. No one had clothing that fit quite right. The younger girls and boys in the family wore their older sibling's hand-me-downs whether they fit or not. The older children wore either church donated clothing or clothing that could be purchased at Sally's.

Helen was a tomboy of sorts. She was petite and pretty, but gritty. As a child she always wanted to play and rough house in the streets with her brothers and their friends. Rather than do the typical chores of sewing, cooking, or cleaning that her sisters did, she much preferred to collect old crates at the Coty cosmetics factory on the West Side and chop scrap wood for the pot belly stove in the apartment for times when they ran short of coal or couldn't afford to buy it.

Helen, age 10 and her brother John, age 2, 1935.

Helen learned at a young age how to be industrious. When she was ten years old, she wanted to get a job. She was too young to get a real job anywhere and jobs were tough to come by anyway in the '30s. Some places wouldn't hire girls because so many men were out of work. The men needed the jobs to support their families.

A treat for Helen when she was a kid was going to the movies to see a double feature plus the news reels for the price of admission. Other than playing in the street and going to Central Park, it was the only entertainment she had. The movies cost a dime, although sometimes it was cheaper in the rear balcony seats known as peanut and popcorn heaven. Ten cents was a lot of money for a kid and Helen's mother never had movie money to give her or her brothers and sisters.

Helen would make the rounds to a bunch of neighbors, especially the ones on the upper floors of the buildings on her street and offer to run to the grocery store or do some other errand. She could usually find at least five neighbors who didn't want to go up and down four or five flights of stairs and they would give her something to do. When Helen came back with their groceries or maybe some food from the bread lines or the soup kitchen at the local church, she was paid a penny. She considered that a pretty good deal for a kid.

Although Helen and her neighbors were poor, there were still people in New York City who had money. Once she earned five pennies, she bought five shopping bags and walked over to the fancy stores on Fifth Avenue or down to Macy's on 34th Street. She'd sell the shopping bags for two cents each to women entering the stores on Fifth Avenue or who were going to shop at Macy's. Helen stood on the sidewalk in front of the doors and called out, *Strongest shopping bags in the city. You'll need 'em for today's sales.* By the time the afternoon was over, she had pedaled all of her shopping bags and doubled her money.

Helen earned that dime with relative ease. She could fly up and down four or five floors worth of stairs faster than anyone she knew. She could take the trip up at almost a dead run leaping over every other step, elevating herself two stairs at a time. For the flights of stairs going down, the sight of her feet was a blur as she raced down the steps at a reckless pace. The last flight was the quickest of all as she always hopped on the slippery bannister and rode it to the ground floor. If her mother ever spotted her gliding down the bannister, especially in a skirt, she was chastised for not acting ladylike. Being ladylike was of little interest to Helen.

Another form of entertainment for children in the tenements was climbing out of a bedroom window and hanging around with your brothers, sisters, or other kids in the neighborhood on the fire escape, playing cards, talking with friends or simply escaping the stifling heat in the apartment during a sweltering summer evening. At the age of eight, Helen was out on the fire escape with her sisters one day. Helen was never one for sitting in one place for an extended period of time. She was in a state of constant motion. Her sisters Mary and Catherine sat and chatted on the fire escape's platform while Helen climbed the ladder that extended up toward the roof of the building. After reaching the top of the ladder, she tried to lower herself back down to the wrought iron fire escape landing just outside their apartment window. Helen slipped and fell over the fire escape rail, plummeting toward the concrete sidewalk below. Mary and Catherine gasped as their little sister plunged downward, her life in jeopardy.

As she hurtled over, her leg caught on a sharp metal protrusion extending out from the fire escape platform on the floor below. While that stopped her from falling to the sidewalk, and most likely to her death, a long, deep gouge of the flesh on her lower leg opened as she dangled four floors above the pavement below. Her fall, being temporarily arrested, allowed Helen to grab onto a rail on the fire escape as she wailed in pain and cried for help. A slip of her hand or the tearing away of her leg would result in a fatal fall.

Her sisters screamed and Helen's brother Marty appeared at the apartment window. He was stunned and froze at the sight of his little sister dangling from the fire escape. Blood oozed from her butchered leg. He leaped through the open window onto the fire escape, scrambled to where Helen hung and pulled her up to safety. Helen's mother then appeared at the apartment window. Cradled in her brother's arms, Marty passed Helen through the window to her mother who laid her on the nearest bed.

"Dear God. What a bloody mess," Maggie said at the sight of Helen's shredded skin, ripped flesh, and torn muscles. The gash was so deep, her tibia was exposed.

Maggie tried to wipe away the blood, but as quickly as she wiped, the blood kept pouring out. Marty and Maggie wrapped and tied a towel around her badly wounded leg as tightly as they could to try and stop or slow the bleeding.

"Marty, you have to get Helen to the hospital. Now! She may bleed to death."

Marty picked Helen up again and underneath her, the bed sheets were a sea of red. He made his way out of the apartment, across the hall and headed down the stairs. In his wake, he left a crimson trail. Marty was fift en years old, but was a tall, athletic young man. He quickly negotiated the five flights of stairs of the apartment building with Helen in his arms. Sweat poured from his head and soaked through his t-shirt as he barreled through the apartment building exit and rushed along the street headed to Saint Mary's Hospital two blocks away.

By the time they reached the emergency room of Saint Mary's, it was difficult to tell who the injured party was. Marty was panting breathlessly. His white shirt and khaki pants were splattered with Helen's blood. The nurses directed Marty to put Helen on a gurney. They placed a tourniquet on her mutilated leg just above the wound and rushed her down the corridor to a treatment room. Marty was told to stay in the waiting area.

"Where's my brother?" Helen cried as she was whisked away.

"You'll be okay, Helen," Marty shouted. "I'm staying. I won't leave here without you. Mom is on her way."

Helen laid on the gurney in the emergency department treatment room surrounded by stained curtains and the smell of sickness. She was given a shot of medication for pain. A doctor and nurse got her bleeding under control. After the preliminary examination of her leg, Helen overheard the whispers of the doctor and nurses discussing the severity of her injury.

"It's pretty bad."

"Do you think you can save her leg, doctor?"

"I don't know. We'll try."

There was a possibility that Helen's leg might be amputated. Although the thought of losing her leg was frightening, the notion ran through her head that she might be excused from ever attending school again if she only had one leg. She hated going to school so much that she thought the loss of a leg might be an equitable trade if she were able to permanently evade school attendance.

As she was wheeled into a dimly lit room and the reality of a lost limb began to sink in, so did panic. Within this small room two people moved the gurney on which Helen rode across the black and white checkered linoleum floor and next to a hard, cold table. They lifted Helen off of the gurney, placed her on the table and instructed her to lie perfectly still. A large machine was then placed a few feet over her leg. A sharp beam of light in the shape of a cross, shined down on her wound. Helen was convinced that the machine was going to come down like a guillotine and chop off her leg. A nurse saw a look of terror on the little eight-year-old girl's face. Helen had tears streaming from her eyes.

"You look so scared," the nurse said to her. "We gave you some medicine for your pain. Does your leg still hurt a lot?"

"I don't want to have my leg chopped off."

"Oh honey, don't worry," the nurse said in a comforting voice. "This is an x-ray machine. We're not cutting your leg off. We're just taking a picture of it. It won't hurt a bit. I promise."

Helen didn't lose her leg. Although she despised attending school as much as ever, she was grateful to have the ability to walk there each day. Dozens of stitches, plenty of rest and a few weeks of walking with crutches was all that she needed. Within a few months she was back hanging around on the fire escape and playing Ring-O-Levio, Stoop Ball and Johnny-on-the-Pony with her brothers and the other kids on the street.

As Helen and her siblings grew, they found many ways to entertain themselves. Since they rarely had carfare to get around the city, when they didn't want to walk or their destination was far across town, they snuck free rides. When they lived on 36th Street, horse drawn wagons traveled back and forth on the street headed to and from the silk houses. The silk houses across the street from their apartment were businesses where men's suits were made. The wagons delivered the material to make the suits and transported the completed product to men's clothing stores and department stores around the city. Helen and her brothers tried to sneak onto the wagons to get a free ride to their destination. Sometimes they just rode for the fun of it. Sneaking a ride on the trolley provided an occasional free trip as well.

The horsemen on the silk wagons and the drivers and conductors of the trolley cars weren't enamored with free-loaders. Regardless of age, if a trolley driver spotted someone sneaking a ride, he would intentionally speed up or stop erratically to shake a free-loader off. It didn't matter whether someone fell off or how badly a kid was hurt, the driver just kept on going.

Once the kids were old enough and had a little money to buy an old pair of metal roller skates or get a pair of hand me down skates to strap to their shoes, they snuck up behind a stopped trolley, bus, or wagon, grabbed ahold of a rear bumper and got themselves an exciting free ride. The bumps, bruises, injuries, or even an admonishment from the neighborhood cop, never dissuaded Helen from the next street game or a new adventure.

1860's • 1870's • 1880's • 1890's • 1900's • 1910's • 1920's • 1930's • 1940's

↑

1865-1937

An Ohio Boy's Roots

"Where is the boy to whom the call of the wild
And the open road does not appeal?"
—Robert Baden Powell

Clarence Raymond Stephenson, Jr. was born November 8, 1920 in the family's South Fifth Street home in Ironton, Ohio. Ironton is a small, rural city of ordinary folks near the southern tip of Ohio, just across the murky waters of the Ohio River from Kentucky and West Virginia.

While Helen's people were recent arrivals to America, Raymond's roots in Ohio went back generations. His ancestors lived on a houseboat on the Ohio River, a boat they built with their own hands. As many as thirteen family members at a time called that boat and the river home. The family supported itself by fishing the river and supplying markets with fish.

Raymond's great-grandfather, Calvery Stephenson, fought for the Union Army during the Civil War. Raymond's favorite childhood stories were about his Great-grandpa Stephenson and his service in the war between the North and South. A long history of struggles and hardships for the Stephenson family goes back to when Calvery Stephenson left his wife and children behind on their family farm to fend for themselves, as he went off to fight to preserve The Union. The family had two horses on the farm. While both were good, strong field animals, one was a capable swimmer and could readily cross a river. Calvery had the wisdom to train the other horse to avoid and fear the streams and rivers that bordered the lands around the family farm. He figured that if the horse ran off or was stolen, it wouldn't get too far. Calvery took the river-worthy horse off to war with him and left the other, so his wife could use it to till the farm fields.

During Calvery's absence, a cadre of Confederate soldiers came to the family farm. They helped themselves to the Stephenson family crops in the fields, and then raided the kitchen cupboards, taking what food was available. Their slamming of the cupboard doors brought the children to tears. Fearful of what retribution she and her children might face if the southern soldiers knew her husband was a Union Army soldier, she told them that her husband had ridden off to purchase some supplies and she wasn't certain when he would be back. The Confederate soldiers decided to take the sole remaining horse. Calvery's wife begged them to leave the horse since it was the only animal she had to work the farm. The unsympathetic Rebels laughed, confiscated the horse and took their leave.

Within an hours' ride of the Stephenson farm, the Confederate soldiers came upon a river that they had to forge to reach their destination. Calvery trained that horse well, because no amount of cajoling, pleading, coercing, or whipping would convince that horse to place so much as a single hoof into the water. The Confederate soldiers, concerned that Union soldiers might be in pursuit, grew impatient and abandoned the obstinate equine. The horse managed to find its way back home on its own. Calvery Stephenson, although not a formally educated man, had a more useful attribute, horse sense.

Raymond's grandfather, Sherman Stephenson, spent most of his life on the family's houseboat on the Ohio River. He was a man of many self-taught skills having served as a fireman, construction foreman, steam engine operator, sawmill operator, and an engineer at the Alpha-Portland Cement Company in Ironton.

By the late 1800s vaccines had become available to folks in the Ironton area to ward off some highly infectious and debilitating or deadly diseases. Sherman didn't believe in the power and preventative properties of vaccines and refused to be injected with them. His obstinacy proved to be fatal as smallpox swept through the city and Sherman, unprotected, contracted the insidious disease and died at the age of thirty-six. Surviving him was his wife and their four children, including Raymond's father, who was just a boy when his father died. With Sherman's passing, the family was forced to abandon the houseboat and life on the river to settle in Ironton.

The city of Ironton was founded in 1849 by John Campbell, a prominent iron manufacturer. He became interested in the lands that surrounded the place that would eventually bear the name Ironton, because of its rich iron ore content. The cost efficient manner in which this valuable commodity could be mined and the ease with which the ore could be moved across the terrain, as well as the proximity of Ironton to the Ohio River for shipping, made this location ideal for manufacturing iron related products.

In the mid to late 1800s Ironton was one of the world's largest producers of iron. America's first iron clad ship, the *USS Monitor*, was constructed from iron produced there. The European powers of France, England, and Russia purchased and used Ironton's most precious resource for the construction of warships due to its exceptional quality and durability.

Immense wealth poured into Ironton because of the success of the iron industry. Ironton's growing prosperity, the expansion of the railways, an active port for exporting on the Ohio River, and the influx of new people, also brought with it exquisite Victorian homes and elegant new churches of many faiths.

By the turn of the century though, the demand for iron had declined and mining the ore, now available only at deeper levels below the surface of the earth, dramatically increased the cost and time of extraction and production. The nation was making a transition to steel as the metal of choice in manufacturing, driven by the burgeoning automobile industry. The softening of the iron industry, combined with the impact of the Great Depression and two devastating floods along the Ohio River, didn't bode well for the once thriving city. As the iron industry declined, Ironton had little with which to replace it.

Despite its economic challenges and a declining population, Ironton was still a city rich in local history, patriotism, and pride. Ironton was part of the Underground Railroad and served as a conduit and safe haven for passage of the victims of slavery making their way north to freedom. It was home to two Medal of Honor recipients who served in the Civil War and Ironton produced the pilot with the second highest number of air combat victories in World War I. It gave more than its fair share of young men who made the ultimate sacrifice in uniform in the service of their country.

After Raymond's grandfather contracted smallpox and passed away, his widow worried about how to keep a roof over the family's heads. She took her children, together with what little savings she had and the proceeds from the sale of their houseboat, and on a cold, cloudy fall morning, stood at the corner of Sixth Street and Neal Avenue where an Ironton city auction of foreclosed properties took place in 1902. She managed to acquire a home where she raised her family.

Raymond's father stayed in school until his second year of high school. He dropped out to find work to help his mother put food on the table and keep up their small, simple, wood-framed home. He became a surrogate father to his younger siblings and made sure they stayed in school. He worked at odd jobs for about one year until deciding to learn the carpenter's trade. Clarence was gifted with his hands and quickly mastered the skills of a woodworker. That talent supported his mother and siblings and eventually his own wife and family. Folks in town said he was an artist with wood. While most of his work involved building and repairing homes, he also designed and built furniture that could grace the rooms of the finest homes.

Clarence's carpentry career was interrupted for one year when his sense of patriotic responsibility compelled him to enlist in the army in order to combat the German forces in Europe during World War I. He was engaged in the military offenses in France at Argonne, St. Mihiel, and Verdun. He was fond of telling a story about German attempts to bomb and destroy the supplies and horses over which he and his unit had charge while in France. Private Stephenson continuously moved the horses and supplies as the German army pelted their location with explosives. The soldiers in his unit followed Clarence as he pursued a pattern of relocating to a spot that had been previously pounded by the enemy, figuring that lightning wouldn't strike twice. Although explosions surrounded them and landed darn close, not a single soldier or horse was lost.

Shortly before the Armistice ended the war, Clarence became quite sick with an unknown illness and was hospitalized in France. He was honorably discharged and sent home in 1919.

He returned to Ironton after the war and married his sweetheart, Miss Marjorie Merle Stewart. Merle, as she was called, was born in 1896 and had deep roots in Ironton herself. Her grandfather served as a member of the Board of Commissioners for Lawrence County from Ironton and her father was one of the early settlers. He traveled alone by horseback along wooded trails when he first came to the area from Pennsylvania. He ultimately settled in southern Ohio with his sixteen year-old bride.

Until her marriage in 1919, Merle spent most of her life on her family's Ohio farm. In addition to working on the farm, she taught lessons in a one-room schoolhouse. Although teachers received a pittance in compensation, that job helped

provide a welcome supplement to the family's income from the financially struggling farm.

Raymond was the first born of Clarence and Merle's three children. In 1922 when Raymond was two years old, his sister Marjorie was born. Six years later another sister, Ruth, was added to the family.

Raymond was the most adventurous and mischievous among the three siblings. His dad got

Raymond at 6 months of age, 1921.

him out and about early and often. Using his carpentry skills, Raymond's father built a special seat affixed to the handlebars of his bicycle. He plopped Raymond into it as an infant and rode throughout town with him cradled on the handle bars. Raymond walked for the first time at only eight months of age and gave every indication of developing as quite a precocious child.

He first asserted his sense of adventure in concert with his strong walking ability when he was three years old. Despite his mother's insistence that he stay close to their house when playing outside, he decided one day that he'd wander off away from home. Once Merle discovered that Raymond had meandered away, she frantically looked for him around town and solicited the help of her friends and neighbors in her search for him, but to no avail. Toward the end of day as dusk came, Raymond decided he would return home rather than continue roaming from hiding place to hiding place around town. His grumbling tummy was calling him home. At about the same time that Raymond made his way home, his father was arriving there too after a long day of work.

Young Raymond spotted his father heading toward their house on South Seventh Street. Knowing he would likely be in a heap of trouble, he ran up to his father, threw his arms around his legs, and displayed an ingratiating smile.

"Hi, Daddy. I missed you so much! I was looking for you."

Raymond's father stared down sternly at him.

"I'll say hi back, right after you get your spanking."

Raymond never wandered away from home again.

The ages of five and six were a pair of difficult years for Raymond. On his fifth birthday he contracted the measles. Six months later the chicken pox struck. Shortly thereafter, he came down with rubella and then pertussis or whooping cough, which at the time accounted for thousands of deaths each year. Despite the run of bad health, Raymond emerged no worse for wear.

As the economy of Ironton deteriorated during the 1920s, carpentry work became scarce. Circumstances were so bad that the family could not afford gasoline for the car nor food to fill the children's stomachs. A relative owned a small market in Ironton and agreed to sell the Stephenson family food on credit. The thought of doing that was unthinkable to Clarence. He didn't believe in having debt or being obliged to anyone. The home in which they lived he built himself. He bought material as he could afford it and drove every nail, installed every inch of wiring and every foot of pipe himself. Every stick of framing and the plastering of all of the walls were done with his own two hands. He had to put his personal objections to debt and his pride aside, though, in order to feed his family. He vowed that when times got better, he would pay every penny owed.

Raymond's father gathered up his wife and three children and left their home in Ironton to move to Akron, where he was able to find work. The rubber industry was emerging there. Job opportunities expanded in Akron and newcomers wanted to build homes. It was an ideal opportunity for someone with Clarence's carpentry skills.

When the Stephenson family first relocated to Akron, they stayed with relatives, but eventually rented places to live in various locations in and around the city over the next year and a half. The adjustment from Ironton to Akron wasn't easy for young Raymond. He attended three different schools; all of them considerably larger than the Whitwell School he attended back home. Raymond was somewhat quiet as well, which, in addition to frequent moves, was an impediment to making new friends. Despite the family's impoverished state and frequent moves, Raymond maintained an optimistic outlook. He even joked about how poor they were claiming that he was so broke, he couldn't afford to pay attention.

Raymond on the porch of the Stephenson's Ironton, Ohio home, 1928.

After a bit more than eighteen months away, Raymond's father was able to secure a job working on a highway crew near Ironton. The work was back-breaking while laboring under the blistering summer sun, but it was a steady job and allowed the family to return to its roots in Ironton. Clarence supplemented that income with sporadic carpentry work either making furniture or fixing up old homes. Raymond was excited to be back home in the company of his friends and reunited with his favorite teachers. Although she wasn't fond of dogs, Merle allowed Raymond to take in a shivering, starving little stray dog that showed up on their front porch. He named it Pete. It was the cap on his homecoming. Raymond slept better that first night home than he had slept in more than a year.

Raymond didn't have a strong interest in sports as a youngster. He played ball with his friends a bit, but his three favorite pastimes were reading, drawing, and bike riding. He loved drawing ships and castles. He also drew comic characters he dubbed, *Wash Tubbs, Salesman Sam, and Freckles*. He developed an inward creative spirit that was his refuge during periods of prolonged illness and extended absences from home. He found stability in his imagination.

His sister Marjorie was more than a sibling. She was one of his closest companions. She and Raymond rode their bikes together often. Once they packed a lunch and decided to ride up-stream along the Ohio River on the old state highway for thirty miles and once there, eat lunch and ride back. They made it home just in time for supper some eight hours later. Their mother didn't take kindly to her children not being at the table on time for supper and they'd likely go unfed and admonished. The Stephensons had a very large tree in their back yard on which Raymond and Marjorie played Tarzan and Jane. Raymond was real good at that Tarzan jungle yell.

Marjorie was a smart young lady and had skipped a grade in elementary school. Her mother didn't want her to get too full of herself and told Marjorie that the reason some children got to skip a grade was because of the depression and the hard times. Schools were pushing students ahead a grade so that they could save money by teaching and feeding them for fewer years.

Marjorie and Ruth looked up to and admired their older brother. When Dad wasn't around or when the three Stephenson kids were at school or out playing, Raymond watched over them in the same paternal fashion.

Although the family's economic picture had gotten a bit brighter after returning to Ironton, Marjorie and Ruth were reminded daily of their plight as they always had holes in their shoes. Their father cut thin wood inserts or cardboard fillers to fit inside to cover the holes. The family enjoyed riding bikes together, going for hikes in the countryside near their home, and playing cards. Marjorie was particularly fond of a game they called *The Dancing Table*. The family would place their hands flat on the surface of a table and mutter the words *up table*. Marjorie believed that they willed the table to move and dance on the floor by their intentions. No knees, no feet, no tricks, no kidding. It really was magic.

Raymond's best buddy was his cousin Jack Bradshaw. The two of them spent school vacations playing in Jack's family barn on the Bradshaw farm out in the country. They went swimming in a nearby creek and they loved getting into their Uncle Bert's coal mine and some of the old iron mines when the men weren't working there.

Raymond's dad was the Scout Master of Boy Scout Troop 5 of Ironton. Raymond joined the troop at the age of eleven. His father was also a Sunday school teacher at the First Baptist Church. Raymond's mother and father had been raised with a strong belief in God and service to others. They were intent on imparting those attributes on Raymond and his sisters.

As Raymond entered his teen years, he blossomed into an outgoing and confident young man. Rather than isolating himself with his reading and drawing as he had in his younger years, he grew to love the camaraderie of his scouting companions. He joined the Ironton High School Band and became more active in team sports such as basketball and baseball. He loved to run and swim.

Raymond thought his swimming skills might be put to good use in 1937. A combination of an early thaw and historic rainfall caused the Ohio River to crest over its banks in January of that year. The flood devastated the lands and communities adjacent to the Ohio River. Along a stretch that in-

Downtown Ironton, decimated by the flood, January 1937.
(Courtesy of Briggs Library, Ironton, OH)

cluded Pennsylvania, West Virginia, Ohio, Kentucky, Indiana and Illinois, more than one million people were left homeless and nearly four hundred people lost their lives. There was more than a half billion dollars in property damage. It was the wettest month in the recorded weather history of Ohio.

Raymond's family lived about a half-mile east of the river and the water started coming into their house on a Friday morning. It came up into the basement from the sewer pipes. By Friday evening it was up so far that they had to move their fruit jars and anything else that could be spoiled or damaged out of the basement. On Sunday the water was all around the house and no one could go out any farther than the front porch. By Monday, the family moved upstairs to the second floor after putting their piano and stove up on saw horses to try and save them from the rising waters of the river. Raymond wrote afterword in a school report, *School was delayed... on account of the flood. We had thirty-three and a half inches of*

Center Street, Ironton, January 1937.
(Courtesy of Briggs Library, Ironton, OH)

water in our house. We had to stay upstairs. The entire family of five, Raymond, Marjorie, Ruth, and Mom and Dad, as well as two friends of the family, were sequestered to the second floor of their small house for nearly three weeks.

With no heat, the children climbed out of an attic window on sunny days and sat on the roof of the house to get warm. Their father built a row boat that he made by disassembling his work bench, re-cutting the boards and shaping them to make the boat. He tied it to the side of the house. He lowered himself into the boat from the water logged house and rowed to a bakery that had escaped the flood. There he bought bread and buttermilk. A flood covering most of Ironton was one more unexpected hardship. There was no flood insurance and no one to step in to clean up the mess and fix the homes. The Stephensons, like most folks of the times, were on their own. After all the family had been through, they figured it couldn't possibly get worse than this.

1860's • 1870's • 1880's • 1890's • 1900's • 1910's • 1920's • 1930's
↑
1920's–1930's

Hell's Kitchen

Hell has a mild climate.
This is Hell's Kitchen.

—Dutch Fred

Hell's Kitchen was Helen's neighborhood. It spanned from 34th Street up to 49th Street and from 8th Avenue west to the Hudson River in Manhattan. There are many stories about how the area got its name. The first attribution was given to Davey Crocket, who purportedly once described the Irish residents of this section of the West Side.

"In my part of the country (Kentucky), when you meet an Irishman, you find a first rate gentleman; but these are worse than savages; they are too mean to swab Hell's Kitchen."

On September 22, 1881, a New York Times reporter who was following a story on a multiple murder case in a tenement on 39th Street and 10th Avenue, described the building as *Hell's Kitchen* and wrote that this neighborhood was, *probably the lowest and filthiest in the city.* Yet another version of the origin of the dubbing of Hell's Kitchen is that of a New York City cop, Dutch Fred. He was watching a small riot with his rookie partner.

"This place is hell itself," the rookie claimed.

"Hell has a mild climate," Fred responded. "This is Hell's Kitchen."

Helen always figured it was called Hell's Kitchen because it was hot as hell during the summer, or that for the most destitute in the neighborhood during the hard times, it was a living hell. At one end of Helen's block was Sacred Heart Church and at the other, Sheehy's Pub, one of New York's finest Hibernian dives. In between were rows of multi-story tenements. It seemed a proper setting for a neighborhood dominated by poor and working class Irish Catholics to have a Catholic Church at one end of the block and an Irish pub at the other. For a time, Sheehy's was the secret watering hole for New York Yankee slugger Babe Ruth and boxing legend Jack Dempsey, both of whom Helen spotted a time or two making their way to or from the pub.

Helen hated school. She was a constant challenge to the nuns who taught her at St. Michael's and Sacred Heart Schools.

She spent considerable time in the principal's office. She was never openly disrespectful to the sisters, but her interest in studying and completing homework assignments was limited. On one occasion when summoned to the principal's office, a nun displayed a cat o' nine tails while warning Helen about her school work. Although she didn't get a whipping that day, Helen wasn't going to take any more chances. She made every effort to avoid visiting the principal's office again.

Helen Gregg's
First Communion, 1932.

Life in Hell's Kitchen during the late 1920s through the early 1940s was tough. For Maggie Gregg and her children, they were burdened with an additional element of struggle. Helen was about ten years old when Pop's mannerisms and behavior became strange. He wandered from one end of the apartment to the other mumbling to himself. For hours at a time he stared out one of the apartment bedroom windows, looking down at 47th Street five floors below. He had a faraway look in his eyes, as though he wanted to escape from himself and jump out that window. It wouldn't have surprised Helen if he actually did. Pop often smoked a pipe as he ambled about the apartment. He struck stick matches randomly on the walls and then after igniting his tobacco; tossed the still lit match on the floor. It was a miracle that he never set the place on fire.

Maggie and her son Marty, who had taken up the mantle of "man of the house" as his father's dementia worsened, did their best to care for and control the behavior of their husband and father, but to no avail. Pop was hospitalized several times in the psychiatric unit of New York City's Bellevue Hospital. The family was hopeful that Pop would get better as a result of his treatments and hospital stays. For a time that was the case after returning home from a hospitalization. However, his odd behavior would eventually reoccur. As the years went by, his condition worsened in spite of his treatments. Maggie had little faith in modern medicine and was very skeptical of prescription drugs. She threw away any medications that accompanied her husband after a hospitalization.

It seemed after Pop lost his job as the building janitor and then lost subsequent positions as an elevator operator and a hotel doorman, he also lost his spirit. What kind of a man could not hold a job or find a new one? This was the basic definition of a man. The father was the one responsible for earning a living and supporting his family. How could you face your wife, children, neighbors and friends while being such a failure as a man, husband, and father? This wasn't an unusual sentiment for the chronically unemployed during the Great Depression.

What bothered Helen the most was not Pop's behavior, but times when other kids might come by the apartment or see Pop on the street. Some of them would mimic or mock him. It made Helen so mad that she just wanted to beat the living hell out of those little bastards, and a time or two she did. Even if she got the worst of the fight, it still made her feel good. People didn't think that Pop was all there, but she could see the hurt on his face when someone made fun of him.

Pop's sister, Annie Gregg, who also emigrated from Ireland, lived with the family for a time. At some point Annie unexpectedly moved out of the apartment and disappeared. Word got to the family through a friend several months later that Annie was destitute, sick, and hospitalized. She was on Welfare Island, a two mile long, narrow body of land in the East River between Manhattan and the borough

Waiting on a bread line in the Bowery District of New York City.

of Queens.

Welfare Island was the location of a New York City hospital for the mentally incompetent and the impoverished who were seriously ill. Maggie told her daughter Helen and son Martin that they should go to the Welfare Island Charity Hospital to see if their aunt was there and if so, why. They took a ferry across the East River from Manhattan one day in search of Aunt Annie. It was sometime during the late 1930s. Annie was indeed there. Helen and Marty were told she had contracted smallpox. They were permitted to see her and were directed to a dormitory style room where women occupied several rows of beds. Annie was not conscious when they saw her. Other than a sheet and a rough wool blanket, she had nothing on. Her bones were visible through her withered arms. The place smelled putrid and the atmosphere, not one of recovery and restored health, but death. That was the last time anyone in the family saw or heard from Annie. She died at the Welfare Island Charity Hospital at the age of sixty-two, destitute and alone.

With the household's primary bread winner mentally incompetent and frequently hospitalized, everyone in the family did what they felt they needed to do to support their mother and the rest of the family. Helen told her mother she was dropping out of high school at age fifteen.

"I'm smart enough to find work, Mom."

"It's not enough just to be smart, Helen," Maggie scolded her daughter. "You need a diploma now-a-days to prove it."

"You can't eat a diploma, Mom."

Helen took any jobs she could; waitressing, reloading food machines at the Horn and Hardart's Automat, as an usherette at a movie theater, and packing boxes at the Coty

Cosmetics factory. On the way to and from work she picked up deposit bottles from the sidewalk and street. Most were two-centers, but Helen hit the jackpot once in a while with a five- or ten-center.

It didn't seem that anyone in the Gregg family had an easy time of it. Helen's oldest sister Mary was a victim of unspeakable domestic violence. She had married a young man by the name of Albert Savaried, who had convinced Mary and the entire Gregg family by his attire and his knowledge of the Navy that he was a sailor. At some point in time though, they suspected that he was not in fact a sailor, but more likely a common thief and street thug. He was never deployed during the war and every time he made his presence known at the Gregg apartment, some money, food, or household item went missing.

Mary and Albert had a son together, Albert Jr. Shortly after their son was born, Albert began to show overt signs of anger and hostility toward Mary. In time, he began to beat her. His abuse was physical and emotional. He tormented her with uncontrollable outbursts of anger, calling her stupid, lazy, and worthless. He told her that if she ever abandoned him, he would track her down and when he found her and their son, he would kill both of them. Despite his threats, Mary packed a bag one day, grabbed her son, and disappeared. Fearing Albert would make good on his threat to kill her and her son, she went into hiding. Her own family had no idea where she was and no one saw her for more than a year. Helen feared that Albert might kill all of them.

Albert terrorized the Gregg family for a time, showing up at their apartment unannounced at all hours of the day and night, searching for Mary and their son. Helen was afraid to sleep. The family was close to Jimmy the cop, the neighborhood policeman who walked a beat almost every day on their block. Helen went to him for help, telling him about Albert. Jimmy told Helen he would put the fear of God into him. The Gregg family never saw Albert again. Word on the street was that Albert had been involved in some criminal activity and died, or more likely had been killed. Helen could sleep peacefully again and Mary returned home to her family.

Life in Hell's Kitchen during the hard times was a gritty existence scratched out on the grimy streets and tenement halls of the West Side of Manhattan. It was a time when the dreams of a fruitful life for many immigrant families went unfulfilled.

1880's • 1890's • 1900's • 1910's • 1920's • 1930's • 1940's • 1950's

↑

1930-1941

Wars at Home and Afar

_____

A gigantic fleet has amassed in Pearl Harbor.
This fleet will be utterly crushed
with one blow at the very beginning of hostilities.
Heaven will bear witness to the righteousness of our struggle.
—Seiichi Ito, Rear Admiral
Imperial Japanese Navy

The Great Depression was the worst economic decline in the history of the United States. Its effects were felt far beyond Hell's Kitchen. World economies collapsed and those lucky enough to have a job were often employed at wages substantially lower than what they would have earned before the Crash of 1929. Not everyone was hurt to the same degree, but most were harmed in one manner or another.

Although it was a much different brand of poverty from what Helen experienced in New York City during the Great Depression, the Stephenson family faced the challenges of an economy in collapse. Ironton, the city known as The Gateway to Ohio, was in serious decline. The entire state of Ohio was particularly hard hit during the Great Depression. By 1932, Ohio's unemployment rate was over thirty-five percent and more than forty percent of factory workers and sixty-seven percent of construction workers were out of work. As the economy grew worse and jobs became scarcer, there was less to do, little to hope for, and not much to look forward to. Although many clung to their faith, even some of the most devout believers questioned the precepts of their lifelong beliefs regarding good intentions and the rewards of hard work.

These economic challenges were especially hard on fathers and mothers trying to care for their families. The role of the male head of household was clear in the 1930s. The father was the bread winner. It was his responsibility to go to work every day, earn a living, and provide for his family. If a man could not fulfill this role, of what value was he? Certainly anyone who gave their best effort could find work somewhere. It had been so through most of the decade of the 1920s, but it wasn't so any longer.

While the unemployed tried to find work, whether on a farm, in a factory, or in any service role, many were greeted at the door of a prospective employer with a sign that noted, *No Help Wanted*, or more specifically, *The Irish Need Not Apply*. There was no hiding your Irish ancestry. Just a few words revealed an accent, a brogue, which all too often was taken as the voice of the lame brained.

A man out of work for a week or two suddenly found himself unemployed for months. Financial resources disappeared. A father might have watched helplessly as his son or daughter shook from the rickets, because there wasn't enough milk to drink or adequate protein in their system. The diligent worker in pursuit of a job could not afford decent clothes or even soap with which to bathe or shave. People who didn't suffer the same fate as the chronically unemployed looked down on them, assuming there must be something wrong with them. They must be lazy, stupid, or both. Once their appearance deteriorated from lack of hygiene, the absence of dental and medical care, as well as severe weight loss from hunger, they were labeled as bums and hobos.

Fundamentalist preachers chided and admonished their unfortunate followers that God was punishing them and their children as well, for the commission of their sins. Too many listened and believed these sanctimonious pulpit pounders, compounding their despair.

It is impossible to say whether Helen's father was chronically unemployed because of mental health issues or if his inability to find and keep a job weighed on him so heavily that he declined into a state of despair and deep depression. He would not have been the only one who fell victim to such a fate. For indeed, that is what he and most of the unemployed were, victims. They were victims of circumstance. They were victims of a boom and bust economy over which they had no control. However, men in America, whether native born or immigrants, did not see themselves as victims. Many must have wondered what was wrong with them that they could not fulfill that most fundamental of responsibilities, earning a wage. Most would have done almost any type of work.

Raymond's father did just that. Although work was scarce, Clarence would not give in to despair. He moved himself and his family from Ironton to other locations around Ohio to find work. Although he was a skilled carpenter and found work occasionally in construction, he also found work in a factory. The work wasn't always steady and there were stretches of time where food could only be gotten on credit, but he managed to make it. He found that the safety nets of the New Deal were slow to make their way to Ironton. Even if it was available, he could not have brought himself to take advantage of it.

It came to be known by many names; relief, public assistance, welfare, and "the dole." The Gregg family's situation was dire. Its household's primary bread winner was in and out of psychiatric care facilities and mentally incompetent. The matriarch of the family was responsible for a brood of eight. The children did what they could to help support the family. Every nickel they earned was turned over to their mother who might give them back a few cents for themselves. The rest went for food, heat, and rent. The girls and boys waited on bread lines and visited the neighborhood soup kitchen to collect enough food to feed everyone. The local churches were a source of clothing and other essentials that the family could not afford. Hundreds of people stood in line for hours to get food.

On some lines there was only soup. A person brought their own pot or kettle to be filled. Timing was important because if you got to the head of the line too soon, only broth or the watery part of the soup that was on the surface was ladled out. The ladle didn't always make it to the bottom of the large pot where the meat, potatoes, carrots and other vegetables sat. If Helen knew the ladler, she asked him to scoop deeper to get more meat and vegetables and he often accommodated her. Other ladlers just told her to get lost.

Lines at other locations had bread or cereal and on rare occasions fresh fruit. Maggie Gregg tried to give each of her children at least a little hot oatmeal before they went to bed to ward off growling stomachs and warm them up a bit before crawling under the blankets for the night. The heat from the coal stove in the kitchen didn't always make its way to the bedrooms at the opposite end of the apartment. There were some winter nights with no heat at all.

Maggie had little choice during the depths of the Great Depression but to apply for relief. The worst aspect of being on relief was the visits by the people from the New York

Home Relief Bureau. Some relief workers made families feel like they should be ashamed to get help. They acted like the recipients were hiding something.

Helen wasn't sure what they thought her family was hiding. They didn't have any money and often went to bed hungry. One case worker told Maggie that all of her children should drop out of school to try and find work. Some case workers weren't shy about moralizing and criticizing the likes of Maggie for irresponsibly having so many children. Was she to be ashamed for devoutly following the tenets of the religion in which she was raised concerning the issue of birth control and procreation? Should she have abandoned the four children from her husband's first marriage? Despite the embarrassment and indignities of being on the dole, they had to do it. If it wasn't for assistance and help from the church, they wouldn't have survived.

Helen's world was generally confined to 47th Street, a few blocks to the north and south and a couple of avenues east of 9th and west of 10th toward the docks along the Hudson River. There was little interest in roaming outside the friendly confines of her neighborhood. She felt safe there. So too did Raymond, 600 miles to the west, in Ironton.

The Greggs, Stephensons, and most Americans were so engrossed with economic survival during the 1930s, that they failed to realize the countries of Europe and the Empire of Japan, once considered remote, were not a safe distance away. The causes for alarm were the expansionary visions of Germany's Adolph Hitler and Italy's Benito Mussolini. Half a world away, Americans knew little about Emperor Hirohito and did not care about Japan's invasion of China. The growth of military personnel, the expansion of military facilities, and the growing inventory and sophistication of weaponry by Germany, Italy, and Japan were hardly noticed. For the third of Americans who were jobless and the millions who were homeless and hungry, shoes under their feet, a roof over their heads, and a meal in their bellies was enough with which to be concerned.

Benito Mussolini came to power in Italy in 1922. Italians regarded him as a leader who brought order to the country and the man who "made the trains run on time." In 1935 he invaded the nation of Ethiopia in west Africa, a somewhat primitive kingdom that attempted to thwart the well-equipped Italian army with spears, knives and muzzle loaded rifles. Other than economic sanctions, the League of Nations did little about this act of aggression. The United States invoked an arms embargo, but that too had little impact on Italy.

Adolph Hitler, an Austrian who was a corporal in the German army in World War I, first attempted to seize power in Germany with his National Socialist Party in 1923. By 1933, a combination of several factors paved the way for Hitler to achieve his goal. Germany suffered high levels of unemployment. Economic despair was rampant. There was fear within Germany's business community of the German Communist Party. These and other factors, including Hitler's charisma and strong oratorical abilities, enabled him to emerge as Chancellor of Germany and the de-facto legally designated dictator. In 1934 when President Paul von Hindenburg died, Hitler was designated *der Fuhrer* (the Leader). In spite of German assurances to the contrary under the Treaty of Versailles after World War I, Hitler rearmed and expanded Germany's military forces.

Japanese generals and admirals, who had controlled government in Japan since the early 1900s, attacked and occupied China's Manchuria province in 1931. In 1933 they initiated additional military incursions into China. Still reeling through the depths of the Great Depression, the United States chose to ignore the actions of Japan and Germany. Even Hitler's clearly established policies of anti-Semitism and European domination elicited only the mildest of political reactions. Hitler was able to advance the adoption of laws that denied Jews German citizenship. Jewish owned businesses were shut down and their assets confiscated. Ultimately the Nazi institutionalization of anti-Semitism led to concentration camps, the construction of gas chambers, and unprecedented acts of genocide.

In 1938 Germany invaded and annexed Austria and occupied the Sudetenland in the northwestern region of Czechoslovakia which bordered Germany. Great Britain's Prime Minister Neville Chamberlain went to Munich and after acquiescing on the issue of the Czechoslovakian seizure, he returned to London to announce, "I believe it is peace for our time… peace with honor." The peace was short lived as Hitler invaded Poland on September 1, 1939.

Official American policy was similar to that at the outset of World War I. On September 3, 1939, President Franklin D. Roosevelt said, "I hope the United States will keep out of this war.

Jewish children imprisoned at the Auschwitz concentratin camp.

I believe it will. And I give you assurances that every effort of your government will be directed toward that end." The attitude of Americans was consistent with their President. Only five percent of respondents to a Gallup poll in 1939 were in favor of declaring war on Germany. Japan, Germany, and Italy formed a political and strategic Axis. It was their intention to conquer and control the world.

Raymond before enlisting in the Army Air Corps, 1940.

Even on Sundays, the Lord's Day, publishers, editors, reporters, printers, and circulation staff at the newspapers had to get the news out. After attending morning services at the First Baptist Church one Sunday, Raymond went to his job at the offices of the Ironton Tribune, helping to get that afternoon's paper out to its subscribers and readers. As he went through his routine in the circulation department he heard a voice bellowing from the editor's office. "Son of a bitch!" Raymond leaped from his chair and ran toward the editor's office along with most of the staff.

Leaning back in his chair, the editor stared at the newswire machine on his desk.

"God help us."

The date was December 7, 1941.

"At 7:55 a.m. this morning at Pearl Harbor, Hawaii, The Empire of Japan delivered a surprise attack on the United States Pacific Fleet," he read aloud from the newswire. Two hours of bombing and strafing by Japanese military aircraft destroyed or heavily damaged twenty-one ships and nearly two hundred aircraft. 2,335 United States servicemen were dead and another 1,143 wounded. Sixty-eight civilians also lost their lives.

Newspapers across the country report the Pearl Harbor attack in Extra editions.

"Listen up, everybody," the editor barked. "We have a special edition to get out today. Let's get after it."

Sixteen-year-old Helen Gregg was helping her mother prepare Sunday supper when her brother Willie shouted from his seat in front of the crystal radio set in their apartment.

"We've been attacked! Mom, everyone, come and listen."

"God be with us. God bless us. God save us," Maggie mumbled as she heard the news of the attack.

The news spread quickly through radio broadcasts, by word of mouth, and by extra editions of newspapers across the country. The day after the attack, President Roosevelt declared war on Japan, stating that December 7, 1941 would be, "…a date that will live in infamy." The actions and attitudes of ordinary Americans changed dramatically as the news of the Pearl Harbor surprise attack and the devastating losses there spread throughout the nation. All across America from small towns like Ironton, to rural areas of America's heartland, and neighborhoods like Hell's Kitchen in the great cities, hundreds of thousands of young men enlisted as soldiers, sailors, and Marines. They and the families they left behind were galvanized in the great task of defeating the Axis powers. No day had ever so unified the country in a common cause.

1880's • 1890's • 1900's • 1910's • 1920's • 1930's • 1940's • 1950's

↑

1942

A Call to Duty

"KEEP 'EM FLYING"
IS OUR BATTLE CRY!
        —Army Air Corps Recruiting Poster

With a declaration of war, Helen said goodbye to two of her five brothers as they enlisted and went off to fight. Two more would enlist in time. They volunteered to serve in the army and do their part to stem the tide of the advancing Axis powers that threatened the United States and the rest of the world.

The first to go was the oldest, Peter. He was a seasoned veteran having fought in the Spanish Civil War on the side of the Nationalists, who had strong Catholic convictions and supported the native Spanish clergy. A devout Catholic and living in Ireland at the time, Peter joined the Nationalist cause in Spain as part of the Irish Brigade. Peter enlisted in the United States Army in 1942. He was a soldier's soldier and refused promotions to stay on the ground in the thick of battle with his fellow G.I.'s. He was an acknowledged sharp shooter and saw action in the North African and European Campaigns, including participation in the invasion at Normandy and the Battle of the Bulge. He was a four time recipient of the Bronze Star.

Marty, who served with the elite 42nd Infantry, better known as the Rainbow Division, was next to enlist and was assigned to duty in Europe. Willie followed Marty and shortly thereafter, their younger brother Joey. Willie and Joey found themselves in the Pacific theater.

Their mother, Maggie, little brother John, the youngest of the eight children, and sisters Helen, Mary, and Catherine were left behind to fend for themselves. They prayed daily that their sons and brothers would come home safely one day. Growing up, Helen witnessed the heartache of families whose loved ones had not returned after their military service. She saw the disfigured bodies of wounded veterans. She watched funeral processions for those who gave their last full measure of devotion to their country.

Helen regularly visited a neighbor who had lost a leg in World War I. He lived in the apartment at the opposite end of the hall from her apartment and she went over some evenings to help him with some of the ordinary tasks of living. She was disturbed by the site of this gentleman removing his wooden leg at bedtime. She cried wondering if her brothers, all of whom with which she had a very close bond, would come back with all of their limbs, if at all.

In January of 1942 at his home in Ironton, twenty-one-year old Raymond Stephenson contemplated where his life was headed. His father tried to teach him the carpentry trade, but Raymond had little interest in it. After graduating from high school, he found what work he could and landed two part-time jobs. He worked in the circulation department of the Ironton Tribune, the local newspaper that he delivered to folks around town as a kid on his bicycle. He also worked for Henrite Products Corporation, a local manufacturer of graphite and molded rubber products.

"Ruth, Marjorie, Raymond," Merle Stephenson called out from the kitchen as her husband sat at the kitchen table reading the afternoon paper. "Supper's ready!"

Ruth and Marjorie bounded down the stairs from their bedroom, but Raymond was nowhere to be found.

"Raymond," his mother called again, this time even louder. Still, there was no response and no appearance by Raymond. "Clarence, would you please see if you can find your son? I thought I saw him headed to the yard earlier."

Clarence went out to the back-yard. A cursory glance about the property revealed no one. As he turned back toward the house, he heard someone rustling in the old tree house in which Raymond and Marjorie played Tarzan when they were children.

"Raymond, is that you up there?"

"Yeah, Dad, it's me."

"Don't you think you're a little old to play in the tree house? Besides, you're holding up supper."

"I just came up here to do some serious thinking for a while, Dad. Seems like I did some of my best thinking here when I was growing up."

Clarence started up the small ladder to the tree house that he built when his children were small. He questioned his son as he climbed.

"So, Raymond, what's on your mind that you need a serious thinking place?"

"Well, Dad, I like working at The Tribune just fine and I know I'm lucky to have a job and a steady paycheck from the Henrite factory. A lot of my friends can't find work at all."

"I feel like there's a but coming right about now," his father interrupted.

"But," Raymond emphasized fulfilling his father's expectation, "ever since the news broke about the attack on Pearl Harbor last month, I feel like there's something more important I should be doing."

"You got any ideas, Raymond?"

"Yes, Dad. I want to fight for our country the way you did in the last war."

Clarence climbed up the remaining few steps of the ladder and squeezed into the cramped wooden structure sitting down next to Raymond.

"Son, I'm proud of my service in the army and respect the notion that you want to serve. You need to understand though, that fighting the enemy in the trenches over in Europe and Japan is no picnic."

"I know, Dad, but I wasn't thinking about fighting from the trenches," Raymond replied as he stared out of a tree house window toward the sky. "I want to be a bomber or fighter pilot and fight this war from the air."

"Son, that job's no piece of cake either. You read the newspaper every day and see the stories about airmen being killed or winding up in POW camps. Besides, what do you know about flying? You've never even been in an airplane."

"I know, Dad. But something in my gut tells me that this is what I was meant to do," Raymond countered.

With a slight tremble in his voice, Clarence counseled his son.

"Raymond, you're my only son and the best friend I ever had. I'd hate to see you go off to war and I would miss you terribly. But, I can see in your face and hear in your voice that your head and your heart have pretty much convinced you that this is your calling. Isn't that so?"

"Yes, Dad. That's it! It **is** a calling."

"Well Raymond, you go on and answer that calling and follow your heart. I remember when you were just a youngster and joined the Boy Scout troop. You always had a special sense about you, your instincts were keen and your decisions were smart. And one other thing I know is that you'd be a darn good pilot."

Raymond reached down, extending his hand to help his father up to his feet. As Clarence straightened up, Raymond put his arms around his father.

"I love you, Dad."

Clarence held his son tightly.

"I love you too, son. Now I think we better get out of this tree and inside for supper before your mother gives both of us a whoopin."

Raymond was fond of adventure and the great outdoors. He was a devoted reader of Zane Grey's and Edgar Rice Burroughs' adventure novels. He had a deep Christian faith and was moved as a youngster by a preacher by the name of O.E. Williams and his evangelical mission. He was baptized in the First Baptist Church of Ironton by the Reverend Roy D. Wood. Their messages of faith, love, and service and the music of choirs and the church orchestra (in which he played the oboe), resonated with him and occupied his soul. His father, the person with whom he was closest, had the most significant influence on his life. Raymond wrote in an assignment during his senior year in high school, *I don't know what my life work will be, but my greatest ambition is to be as good a man as my Dad.*

Following in his father's footsteps, Raymond served as an assistant Cub Scout leader and a Senior Patrol leader for the Boy Scouts. As his father had done in World War I, Raymond

Boy Scout Troop 5 of Ironton.
Clarence R. Stepehenson, Sr. (center, back row) and
his son, Clarence Raymond Stephenson, Jr.
(front row seated, second from right).

now would honor his father, his family, and the country he loved, by volunteering to join the United States Army Air Corps. As a teenager, Raymond was fascinated with airplanes and flying. He couldn't get enough of watching aircraft, studying them, or talking about them. It was no surprise to anyone who knew him that on January 31, 1942, Raymond boarded a bus in Ironton headed to Patterson Air Field in Dayton, Ohio. His mission was to become an Army Air Corps aviator.

Raymond's father brought him to the bus station in Ironton after Raymond said goodbye to his mother and his youngest sister Ruth. Merle could not hold back her tears as she held onto her son on the front porch of their home as he prepared to depart. Raymond was an intelligent, faithful, kind, and polite young man. He was everything that his mother always hoped he would be. Although Raymond was athletic and fit, his mother wasn't sure he was suited for the rigors of military life and combat. He was still her little boy.

Clarence harbored no doubts about his son. The times that they hiked, camped, fished, and worked together assured Clarence that his son was ready. Clarence understood the rigors of battle from his combat service in World War I and knew Raymond could handle it. Raymond's sister Marjorie was living and working in Dayton and would be there to greet him when he arrived. She was a stenographer at the Wright Army Air Field.

Raymond began to keep a diary when he started this new phase of his life. In the small, brown leather-bound book he wrote his first entries:

JANUARY 31

1942. *Left Ironton.* 10:00 A.M. via bus to Dayton to start ball rolling toward my getting into Air Corps. Met Marj. + Aunt Dot 4:00 P.M. Rode an escalator for 1st time at Elders. Went to Stewarts

FEBRUARY 11

1942. The start of a new chapter in my life. Was sworn into the army this day; assigned to 18th Repair Squadron, Patterson Field, Fairfield, Ohio. A.S.N. 15110085. Bunk in gym.

Humbly, he pursued his calling.

1880's • 1890's • 1900's • 1910's • 1920's • 1930's • 1940's • 1950's

↑

1942

The Basics

We have hard work to do
And loads to lift.
Shun not the struggle,
Tis' God's gift.

— Anonymous

Raymond's daily activities were physically challenging and exhausting. Drilling, training and weapons familiarization were part of the everyday routine. Medical tests and vaccinations against typhoid, yellow fever, smallpox and every other life threatening communicable disease one might contract in the United States or in some far off land, turned him into a human pin cushion. His eyes were fixed on one objective, to become an aviation cadet. Raymond got his first chance to achieve that goal on March 17, 1942, when he was given the opportunity to take the Army Air Corps cadet program entry exam. He studied for hours each day. Over and over again he read and recited the test material until he was certain he had mastered all of it.

Raymond and hundreds of fledgling cadets sat at desks dispersed throughout a Patterson Field airplane hangar. For hours they labored over a battery of questions and problems. It felt more like an inquisition than an examination. His nerves became frazzled contemplating the consequences of a deficient grade. So much was riding on each query and puzzle to solve. Despite the cool, late winter air that invaded the hangar, perspiration stained the armpits and back of Raymond's khaki uniform.

Two days later, he was informed that he failed the cadet exam by six points. His consolation prize was a new G.I. field pack from the United States Army. A parachute to strap on his back was more what he had in mind.

Raymond, flanked by his sisters, Ruth (left) and Marjorie. Also pictured is his dog, Pete, March 1942.

Raymond needed to share his disappointment with someone and his sister Marjorie, who lived nearby in Dayton, met him at a neighborhood diner. When Marjorie entered the diner, Raymond had already arrived. She spotted him in his uniform, sitting at the counter, cradling a cup of coffee in his hands. She sat down on the red vinyl covered stool next to her brother. The forlorn expression on his face told her there was a problem.

"What's wrong, Raymond?"

"Everything."

"C'mon now, Raymond. Everything can't be wrong."

"Everything that matters, Marjorie."

Marjorie placed her hand on her brother's forearm as it rested on the luncheonette counter.

"Miss, can I get you anything?" A waitress interrupted.

"Yes, a cup of coffee please and a refill for him."

Marjorie turned her attention back to her brother.

"What happened that's got you so upset?"

"I flunked."

"Flunked?" Marjorie shot back. "You've never flunked anything in your life. What did you flunk?"

"I flunked the pilot cadet program entry exam. I got so nervous. I've never wanted anything so much in my life. I lost my focus."

"Raymond, calm down. Just take it again."

"The Army Air Corps is not big on second chances. My career as a pilot is over before it even got started," Raymond moaned as he slumped over the laminate counter top.

Marjorie spun Raymond around on his stool. They were now face to face. "Raymond, you will find a way to take that exam again. You have to. Beg, plead, whatever it takes."

"You're right, Marjorie. I have to find a way."

Raymond was a self-motivated and diligent individual. If only he could be granted a second chance, he would redouble his efforts and study even harder.

"Marjorie, if I do get another shot at this, I swear, I won't choke a second time."

Raymond spoke with his commanding officer the following day, trying to convince him that he was pilot material. Uncharacteristically, Raymond was granted one final opportunity to successfully complete the test. On his second attempt, he aced it.

Raymond's progress in basic training was slow, but steady. On May 15, 1942 he received his first promotion to the rank of Private First Class. *I'm happy about the whole thing,* the understated soldier wrote in his diary regarding his promotion. He was also quite pleased with the raise he received. His pay soared from twenty-one dollars to thirty six-dollars per month, more than he had ever earned. With his promotion came the first of many transfers. He left Ohio for the first time in his life on May 29, 1942. Raymond, along with twenty-nine other young men, boarded a train in Columbus, Ohio headed east to New York City, the home of the Army Air Corps Technical Training School.

After traveling the rails all night, the cadre of young Army Air Corps cadets arrived at Pennsylvania Station in midtown Manhattan at about 7:00 a.m. on a Saturday. They were greeted by a sergeant from the training school and bused to the Hotel Breslin on 29th Street and Broadway. The cadets were given the weekend to roam about New York City. Raymond was fascinated with New York and lost no time discovering many of the sites for which it was best known. With a few of

Raymond in his Army Air Corps cadet uniform.

his cadet classmates, he visited Yankee Stadium, Central Park, and the Statue of Liberty. Raymond figured he better get to it while he could, because there was no time to waste. After the weekend of his arrival, the serious training and hard work would start.

June 1, 1942 began the first of many months of technical training classes for aspiring pilots. Raymond was moved from the hotel in Manhattan to Mitchell Field, an Army Air Corps facility in Garden City, Long Island, where he was housed in military style barracks. Coincidentally, Raymond's father was stationed for a short time in 1919 just a few miles away at Camp Mills in neighboring Mineola while serving in the army during

World War I. Raymond commuted by train to Manhattan from Mitchell Field to attend classes.

Technical training started with the fundamentals of flight and evolved into an intimate knowledge of military aircraft. Every facet of their design and operation, from engines and controls down to every working part between the aircraft's nose and its tail, would need to be mastered. It was no small task and many who entered this program would not finish it. Primary engines, advanced engines, carburetion, and electrical systems were among the not-so-captivating topics in which Raymond and his cadet colleagues would need to become proficient.

The cadets were also learning about the deteriorating war conditions in Europe and the Pacific. The Nazis and the Japanese military threatened world order. With the deepening involvement of the United States in World War II in both the European and Pacific theaters, a growing concern regarding the future of the world's political and military landscape entered the consciousness of the young men whose mission it was to preserve freedom and protect their country and its people. Among the military staff and civilians at home, stories began to surface about atrocities being perpetrated by the nations of the Axis powers. Millions would take up the cause and among them was a young man from Ohio who made the commitment, swore an oath, and donned a uniform.

Raymond neither wanted nor needed anything to distract him from his mission to defend America as a military aviator. As he and two naval aviator cadets walked together through Manhattan's Central Park on a Saturday afternoon in June, absorbed in thought about his goal, he didn't see the approaching impact with fate awaiting him.

1880's • 1890's • 1900's • 1910's • 1920's • 1930's • 1940's • 1950's
↑
1942

A Convergence of Faiths

All religions, arts and sciences
are branches of the same tree.
—*Albert Einstein*

True to his word, the week after meeting Helen for the first time, Raymond came to pick her up at the family's apartment on June 18, 1942, after his classes at the Army Air Corps Technical Training School had concluded for the day. It was their first official date since their improbable encounter in Central Park. After Raymond's walk up to the fifth floor of the apartment building, he knocked on the door and was greeted by Helen's mother.

"Hello. You must be the boy from Ohio."

"Hello, Mrs. Gregg. I'm Raymond Stephenson. It is a pleasure to meet you. Helen has told me so many wonderful things about you and your family."

Although she had earlier been suspicious about someone who had mooched a nickel from a poor girl he just met in Central Park, the polite and gentlemanly manner in which Raymond introduced himself and his clean cut appearance made Maggie more at ease. She sized him up as a respectful Ohioan. She liked him. Having little education and limited knowledge of the Midwest, Maggie envisioned Ohio as a place similar to the great western frontier. She pictured cowboys herding cattle and Indians roaming the open plains, hunting for buffalo.

Helen came to the door to join them.

"Mom, this is Raymond, the young man I met in the park last week."

"So he is."

Raymond looked over Maggie's shoulder into her apartment.

"You have a lovely home, Mrs. Gregg."

"Thank you, Raymond. Would you like to come in?"

"I would love to, Mrs. Gregg."

Given its rundown condition and tattered furnishings, Helen thought Raymond was just being polite when he complimented her mother on the appearance of the apartment and merely courteous when he said he would love to see the rest of the place.

She worried that if Raymond saw how the family lived and what little they had, he would run for the hills. Pop was back in Bellevue Hospital at the time and even though Helen was never ashamed or embarrassed by Pop, she was relieved just the same that on her first date, she didn't have to explain his behavior to Raymond or pick up the match sticks that Pop scattered about the floor after lighting his pipe.

There was not much to see in the Gregg residence. A coal burning pot belly stove, a small, rickety wooden table, and four wobbly chairs in the kitchen at one end of the apartment. A worn out sofa with a wrinkled, floral print cover tossed over it, two hard backed maple chairs, and a crystal radio set graced a living room that was so small, its limited furnishings consumed it. A row of four beds, separated by shabby curtains and one small dresser with a statue of the Virgin Mary upon it, occupied the bedroom at the other end of the apartment. As Raymond made his way past the series of beds, Maggie saw him brush his hand along the bed that Helen shared with her sisters.

"Helen," Maggie whispered to her daughter as she pulled her aside. "Did you see that?"

"See what, Mom?"

"He brushed his hand along your bed. Only your bed."

"No, I didn't see that, Mom. But, so what?"

"It's a sign. I think he's the one."

Helen accepted much on faith and fate, but Maggie often saw signs. Signs from God. Most times Helen thought her mother's signs were eccentric and far-fetched.

"Mom, Raymond and I should be going now."

"Well, run along then."

"It was a pleasure to meet you, Mrs. Gregg. Thank you for having me at your home."

"Thank you for coming, Raymond. Now off with the two of you. God be with you, God bless you, God save you."

Raymond and Helen headed down the five flights of stairs to 47th Street. They walked the streets of New York City together and talked about their families and what it was like growing up, he in Ohio and she in New York City. Helen loved hearing about what life was like for Raymond as a boy. He told her about his family's roots going back to the Civil War and all about his parents, sisters, friends, and the little city he called home. Helen gasped at his telling of the great flood that chased Raymond's family up to the roof of their home and when they abandoned that home for a time when his father couldn't find work in Ironton.

The city streets buzzed with the sounds of buses and taxis. Teems of people crowded the sidewalks. Apple sellers and boys with the late day newspapers hawked their wares.

"Fresh apples. Two for two cents."

"Extra, extra. Gets your New York Evening Post."

Raymond and Helen sauntered hand in hand. Raymond listened to Helen divulge stories of the hardships her own family endured from their roots back in Ireland to the tenements in New York. She told him about her seven brothers and sisters and about Pop's hospitalizations and problems. As they walked past Sacred Heart Church, she pointed to the area where she stood in the bread and soup lines. Raymond squeezed her hand and she watched his eyebrows rise. She knew he understood that it hadn't been easy for her. She pointed toward the church.

"That's where I go to mass."

"You're Catholic?"

"Of course, Raymond. Aren't you?"

"No. Our family goes to Sunday services at the First Baptist Church of Ironton."

They broke hands momentarily and faced each other.

"Uh oh," Helen said. "My mother is not going to want to hear about this."

"My folks neither."

Raymond reached out, retook Helen's hand, and they continued on, headed toward Times Square. They dropped the subject of their disparate faiths. It didn't matter to them. Actually, not much of anything mattered. Not the poverty in which they lived, not the war in Europe or the battles in the Pacific. All that mattered was that a sweet young lady and a dashing lad in uniform somehow found each other.

"Raymond, there's the automat where I work," Helen said as she pointed toward Horn & Hardart's. Raymond and Helen were hungry and entered the automat to grab a bite to eat. Raymond deposited his change into two vending machines, turned the knobs unlocking the small glass doors, and extracted a liverwurst sandwich and piece of cherry pie for them to share. They sat across from each other at a small aluminum table on metal chairs with red plastic covered seats.

"I don't care, Helen."

"What don't you care about, Raymond?"

"That you're Catholic."

"It doesn't matter to me that you're Baptist."

Famished, they made quick work of their sandwich and pie and headed back toward Helen's apartment. When they arrived at their destination in front of Helen's building, she leaped up onto the second step of the front stoop, with Raymond standing on the sidewalk two steps below. Helen turned around to face him. At five foot, four, Helen was eye to eye with Raymond. She rested her arms on his shoulders as she placed her hands behind Raymond's neck, locking her fingers. She gently pulled him toward her. In anticipation of what Raymond hoped was going to happen, he closed his eyes. Helen likewise closed her eyes and kissed him ever so softly on the lips. Raymond wrapped his arms around Helen and hugged her tightly for a moment. When he released her, she turned without saying a word and darted through the entry way into the apartment building. Helen took the climb up to the top story of their tenement building bounding two steps at a time, but on this occasion, she could have floated all the way to the uppermost floor.

As the late evening air cooled and a breeze scattered some debris about the street, Raymond stood there at the foot of the front stoop, frozen in place. He savored the feeling of having held Helen in his arms. The sensation of her warm, soft kiss still lingered on his lips. Once Helen disappeared from his sight, he peered through the glass doors of the apartment building entrance for a moment and then turned and slowly began walking east toward 9th Avenue.

"Hey Raymond."

He heard an angelic voice as though it was coming from heaven above.

"Up here."

He looked up and through the glow of a street lamp, he saw Helen on the fifth floor fire escape platform.

"When will I see you again?" Helen called down to him.

"Tomorrow and I hope every day for the rest of my life," Raymond shouted back.

"Okay, Raymond."

And with that, Helen climbed back through the apartment window. As she readied for bed, she clutched to the excitement of their first kiss. Maybe Maggie's signs weren't so far-fetched after all.

Raymond walked a mile or so to Penn Station on 33rd Street to board the train to Mitchell Field. Thoughts of Helen consumed his mind for the entire trip back to his barracks. After arriving there, he sat on the coarse, green wool blanket at the edge of his bunk and composed a new entry into his diary.

JUNE 18

1942. First date with Helen Grigg. I've never known a girl like her. Already I'm in love with her.

1880's • 1890's • 1900's • 1910's • 1920's • 1930's • 1940's • 1950's
↑
1942

Summer Paradise

...it was a never-to-be-forgotten summer –
one of those summers which come seldom to any life...
—*L.M. Montgomery*

As the next few months passed, Raymond progressed with his Army Air Corps training and every free moment was time he spent with Helen. Although she was born and raised in New York City, Helen never visited the Empire State Building. She and Raymond decided to take the elevator to the observation deck of the world's tallest skyscraper together. When the elevator doors opened and they stepped out onto the observation deck, the view took Helen's breath away. Above was a blue bird sky. From her perch she saw the rivers that surrounded Manhattan, the sun glistening off the top of the Chrysler Building, and the greenery of Central Park. A cool breeze at that elevation made her shiver. Raymond wrapped his arms around her from behind to keep her warm. Raymond found the views of the New York City skyline, for as far as the eye could see in every direction, striking. He and Helen leaned against the wooden safety rail and marveled at all they saw.

In a city of millions of people, they shared their own private paradise. Posted on the wooden safety rail were signs that warned about the forbidden practice of memorializing one's visit by carving or writing initials, names, or messages anywhere on the observation deck. However, Helen brought a small pocket knife from home for just such a purpose. Compelled by the scenic beauty and their romantic feelings of the moment, she carved their initials, enveloped in a heart, into the rail. They kissed under sunny skies, littered only with a few white, puffy clouds.

"I love you, Helen."

"Oh, Raymond. I'm so excited to hear those words."

Helen stared at Raymond. He was handsome, polite, funny, respectful, and smart. What was not to love about him?

"I love you too, Raymond. I love everything about you."

They shared visits to the Statue of Liberty and many of the museums and other attractions in New York. Helen had been somewhat sheltered and protected by her mother, older sisters, and brothers growing up. She rarely ventured from 47th Street other than to go to work, a movie, or take a walk up to Central Park. Given the family's financial condition, she couldn't spend money frivolously on the subway, buses, or trolley. There was no money for the ferry ride to Liberty Island or admission to venues for which there was a fee to enter.

Helen found it ironic that a small town boy from Ironton, Ohio was the one who introduced her to many of the most interesting and popular sites in her own home town. It didn't really matter where she and Raymond went or what they did though, as long as they were in each other's company.

Their favorite place to spend time together was on the beach at Coney Island in the borough of Brooklyn. Coney Island had an amusement park with rides, circus-style side-shows and food of every variety along its oceanfront boardwalk. Despite the plethora of entertaining activities,

Raymond and Helen mostly enjoyed just sitting on the sands of the beach and wading in the ocean's waters.

On their first visit to Coney Island together, Raymond took Helen's hand and brought her to the water's edge. Helen was a little reluctant, because she didn't know how to swim and wasn't sure just how far or deep into the water Raymond planned to go. As they began to enter the cold water and the gentle surf that day, Helen hesitated.

"How far out are we going?" Helen asked nervously.

"Why?" Raymond asked as he chuckled.

"I can't swim," Helen confessed.

"How about we go in just up to our knees?" Raymond suggested.

"Okay, but no funny business."

Once they waded to the depth of their knees, Raymond turned to Helen and shared a story with her.

"I had a boyhood dream that someday I would travel from Ohio to both the east coast and the west coast of the United States

Helen at Brooklyn's Coney Island Beach.

and stick my feet in the waters of the Atlantic and Pacific Oceans. I never thought that I would be holding hands with the prettiest girl in New York when I stepped into the Atlantic Ocean for the first time."

Raymond pulled Helen close to his side and wrapped an arm around her.

"I'm so happy that I could fulfill the first half of that dream with the girl I love. Someday, you and I will complete the rest of my dream, Helen. We'll drive to California. No, I'll fly us to California and together, we'll go in the Pacific Ocean too."

"I don't want that to be only your dream anymore, Raymond," Helen responded as she turned toward him looking up into his eyes. "From now on, it's our dream."

Raymond wanted to be certain that he and Helen would fulfill that dream and many others together some day. On August 8, 1942, the two of them spent the day in Central Park. They took an old wooden row boat out on the lake in the park and afterward, shared a picnic lunch on a grassy knoll by the edge of the water. As ducks paddled across the tranquil waters of the lake, Raymond and Helen talked about the approaching end of Raymond's training period in New York and how saddened they were at the prospect of parting.

Raymond looked forward to the next phase of training to become a pilot, but that notion was overshadowed by the dread of saying goodbye to Helen. What would happen after he left? Would she wait for him? When would he be able to come back for her? There they were, together in Central Park, not far from the spot where they first bumped into each other a mere seven weeks earlier. Sadly, they realized that in only eight more weeks, Raymond's next assignment would take him away from Helen. There was no telling for certain how long they would be separated.

Raymond thought about this day and this moment frequently over the previous few days. What would be the most romantic place? Should they be sitting or standing? Would it be best to get down on one knee? Raymond and Helen sat on an old woolen blanket that they had spread on the grass overlooking the lake. Helen leaned up against him.

With her head resting on his shoulder and his head tilted ever so slightly toward her, he whispered in her ear,

"Helen, will you marry me?"

"What did you say?" Helen blurted out as her head snapped around to face Raymond.

"I said, 'Helen, will you marry me?' I want you to marry me. Spending the rest of our lives together is the right thing to do. I love you and want you to marry me before I leave New York."

"I love you too, Raymond and I want to marry you, but...."

Raymond's heart sank and he turned away from her with a wounded look on his face.

"But, what? You can't say no."

"I'm not saying no, Raymond. I just can't marry you now."

There was an obstacle standing in the way of a marriage between Helen and Raymond that summer. Helen was only sixteen, a month shy of her seventeenth birthday. She would turn seventeen on September 6, 1942. They had to wait until the following September when Helen would turn eighteen to marry.

"My mother told me and my sisters we could not marry until age 18. Can you please wait, Raymond?" Helen implored.

"I will wait until your 18th birthday or eternity if I have to, darling. But I need to know that someday you will be my wife."

"In that case, Raymond, then yes. Yes. I will marry you."

There was a second possible impediment to a Stephenson and Gregg marriage of which they were both aware, but about which nothing was spoken on their engagement day. How would Helen's devout Irish, Roman Catholic mother and Raymond's fervently committed Baptist mother and father feel about a marriage to someone of a different faith? By whom would they be married, a Catholic priest or a

Baptist minister? Would the ceremony take place in a Baptist or Catholic Church? Would those churches and their clergy marry two individuals of disparate faiths?

Maggie firmly believed that you were not legitimately married in the eyes of The Church or God if not married in a Catholic church by a Catholic priest. It was sinful. There were cultural biases by some Irish Catholics against Protestants due to the long conflict between Catholics in Ireland and Protestants in England and Northern Ireland.

Raymond and Helen went directly from Central Park to tell Helen's mother of their engagement. Helen feared her mother's reaction. This was a woman, who kneeled by the side of her bed every night to pray the Holy Rosary and who attended Holy Mass on almost a daily basis to pray for food for the table, coal for the stove, and for the safe return of her sons from war. She seemed an unlikely candidate for tolerance of an interfaith marriage. Helen had never defied her mother. Raymond told Helen he wanted to speak with his prospective mother-in-law first, alone.

Raymond sat with Helen's mother in the kitchen of her cold water flat. Helen waited in the bedroom at the opposite end of the apartment, eavesdropping.

"Mrs. Gregg, may I speak with you about something very important?"

"Is it about Helen?"

"Yes ma'am."

"What do you have to say for yourself, Raymond?"

"I love your daughter very much. Like you and your family, me and my family are Christians. We share a deep faith in God and Jesus, but we are Baptists. I have a great respect for everyone of faith and I would never ask Helen to forsake her

Catholic upbringing. As much as I love Helen, out of respect for you, I will only marry Helen if I have your blessing."

Maggie believed Raymond was a decent young man who would treat her youngest daughter with kindness and respect. She was confident that he would be a good provider and a good father to their children. She remembered the sign that she witnessed during Raymond's first visit when he touched Helen's bed. She saw love in her daughter's eyes and a new-found happiness that lifted Helen's spirits above the daily despair that enveloped Hell's Kitchen.

Maggie called Helen into the kitchen and sat her down in a chair next to Raymond at the kitchen table. Raymond was perspiring profusely, even though the room temperature couldn't have been more than seventy degrees that evening. Helen's knees knocked below the kitchen table's oak surface. Maggie leaned across the kitchen table, extending one hand to Helen and the other to Raymond.

"Helen, Raymond is a good man. I have had many a good, faithful Protestant as a friend and I can tell you, they have been fine and loyal friends. My life with Pop hasn't been easy because of his illness and all. His life with his first wife was cut short by her death. You have a chance for a long, happy and blessed life together. Nothing should come in the way of that. If you could only allow a priest to preside over your wedding, then you have my blessing."

"As you wish, Mrs. Gregg," he said with deep sincerity. "I love your daughter and will cherish her always." Raymond beamed and squeezed Maggie's hand.

A broad, brilliant smile came to Helen's face. A tear of happiness crossed her cheek.

1880's • 1890's • 1900's • 1910's • 1920's • 1930's • 1940's • 1950's

↑

1942

Parting

And ever has it been known,
that love knows not its own depth,
until the hour of separation.

—Khalil Gilbran

On September 12, 1942, Raymond graduated from the Aviation Institute of Technology. He was promoted to the rank of Corporal and proud that he finished this stage of preparation to become a pilot. However, he was distressed that the Army Air Corps no longer had a reason to keep him in New York and near his cherished Helen. Two weeks later he received orders to leave Long Island's Mitchell Field and return to Patterson Field in Dayton, Ohio.

According to his newest orders, October 10, 1942 would be the last day he might ever see Helen. Despite their engagement, neither of them really knew with certainty when, or if, they would see each other again. The war and the Army Air Corps paid no mind to the whims and desires of young lovers. Raymond and Helen spent his entire last day and night in New York together. So many days and evenings ended that summer and fall with Raymond sitting beside Helen on the front stoop of her tenement building. Here they were again, in the chilly, wee hours of the morning. Raymond's arms surrounded Helen.

"I'm not sure exactly what day and I don't know for sure where it will happen," Raymond proclaimed to Helen before they parted, "but, you and me will get married next year."

"Whenever that day comes Raymond, and no matter where we are," Helen said with equal conviction, "that day will be the happiest day of my life."

The following day, Raymond boarded a train to Ohio. As the train pulled out from the station, he pulled his diary from his duffel bag. With a heavy heart, he inscribed:

OCTOBER 10

19 42— My last evening with Helen. Didn't know if I could get out Sunday or not so we said our last regretful goodbyes about 2:00 AM. I could hardly bear to leave her.

The next day he was back at Ohio's Patterson Field, where he had enlisted eight months earlier to the day. After his arrival, he was processed and assigned to Cadet Squadron E, Group One. Little more than a month later, Raymond had to pack his belongings into a duffel bag and once again board a train, this time headed for the west coast. The trip covered over 2,500 miles of rail from Ohio through Tennessee, Alabama, Louisiana, Texas, New Mexico and Arizona. He finally arrived in December 1942 at Santa Ana, California. He received his barracks assignment, a blanket and a pillow. After finding his bunk, he sat and wrote a letter to his fiancée, Helen.

The typical cadet work day was long and tedious. The bugle sounded reveille at 5:30 a.m. rousting the cadets out of their bunks. They had fifteen minutes to dress, clean up, and get to breakfast in the mess hall. Raymond was his high school band's oboe player and taught himself to play the bugle during what little free time he had. He was called upon occasionally to play reveille, the reward for which was having to get out of his bunk earlier than his fellow cadets.

Breakfast was followed by latrine duty. Afterward, it was on to classroom training followed by calisthenics, military drills, machine gun practice, aircraft familiarization and more training. At the end of a long and exhausting day came supper. But the work-day still was not complete. Cleaning the barracks and other ministerial duties could occupy an entire evening before hitting the sack at 2100 hours. There might be some time in the evening to write letters home and on a rare occasion, watch a movie.

One evening a cadet in Raymond's squad asked their commander if they could skip some evening duties to watch the film, *The Road to Morocco.* The squadron commander's face turned a bright red. Veins bulged from his neck and forehead. He got nose to nose with the cadet.

"You were not sent to the Santa Ana Army Air Corps West Coast Training Center to watch Bob Hope, Dorothy Lamour, and Bing goddamn Crosby on the road to anywhere. You are on the road to Germany or Japan to kill some Nazis or Japs and you better be prepared for it! Do you understand me, cadet?"

"Yes, sir!"

Although Raymond and his fellow cadets had a personal goal to become pilots, few of them had ever been in an airplane. Most soldiers who voluntarily enlisted in the armed forces during World War II were driven in part by patriotism. But, what was it that made these particular soldiers want to fight this war from the sky? For Raymond, he was young and impressionable. He was consumed by the excitement and romanticism of flying and the chance to soar among eagles.

There was no shortage of books, films, and newsreels inducing such notions in young men.

Raymond and the other lads like him, learned in time that the dangers of flying in battle far outweighed the romantic fascination of being airborne. During World War II more than fifteen thousand pilots, bombardiers, gunners, other crew members, and ground personnel were killed in the United States while training. Mechanical failures, inclement weather while in flight, and pilot or navigator errors were among the leading causes of training fatalities.

To say these were merely accidents was to understate their consequences. It was someone's husband, father, brother, or son who perished. Families were irreparably torn apart. A mother mourned the loss of a boy she cherished. A young bride's flame of love and passion was extinguished. Extraordinary risks for flight crews to mitigate and overcome were present even before the enemy started shooting at them.

An endless number of tests were imposed in training. Running tests, tests of physical strength and agility, math tests, physics tests, machine gun accuracy tests, mapping and charting tests, mechanical knowledge tests, tests on ground forces, armored vehicle tests, tests on enemy air forces, and even personal hygiene tests. The thoroughness and frequency of testing weeded out anyone who did not show the aptitude and attitude to be a pilot.

Raymond and his fellow Air Corps cadets got a four-day leave and a break from the challenges and monotony of training for the Christmas holiday of 1942. Raymond wanted desperately to visit Helen in New York and his parents and sisters in Ohio, but there was just not enough time. He had never spent a Christmas away from his family. However, he and a few other cadets, who were also far from home, decided to spend two days in Los Angeles and Hollywood, rather than sit around their barracks feeling sorry for themselves.

Raymond and his colleagues shared a room at the Cecil Hotel in Los Angeles and had a swell turkey dinner Christmas Eve. In addition to seeing the sights around Los Angeles and Hollywood, they took in a few movies including *Woman of the Year* and *Roman Holiday*. Some of the guys went to the beach, but Raymond declined remembering the promise he made to Helen at Coney Island, to set foot in the Pacific Ocean for the first time with her.

The 1942 Christmas holiday for Raymond's seventeen-year-old fiancée was a quiet one back in New York. Helen desperately missed Raymond. Some days she sat by a bedroom window looking at the front stoop of the building five floors below, where she and Raymond shared their first kiss. Her eyes roamed up and down 47th Street, hoping that he would unexpectedly appear. She derived some comfort from the frequent letters she received from him, and by putting pen to paper to send notes to Raymond in return.

The apartment on 47th Street was quieter and less congested than in prior years. Three of Helen's brothers had already enlisted in the Army and a fourth would soon follow. Her sister Mary, who had moved out a year or so earlier, was still nowhere to be found. She and her son were still hiding from her abusive husband who had threatened to kill them. Pop missed this Christmas. He was readmitted to Bellevue's psychiatric ward for treatment. The apartment that had housed a family of ten was now down to less than half of that.

Gifts at Christmas were the same from year to year with the Gregg family now, just as when the children were younger.

Maggie put a fresh piece of fruit in an ordinary stocking that hung from a kitchen shelf. The Gregg children never equated Christmas with the receipt of toys or other gifts growing up. It was a day to celebrate the birth of the baby Jesus in Bethlehem and for family to join together at home and in church.

Despite their poverty-riddled existence, there was always a special turkey dinner for Christmas. Since Helen was betrothed to Raymond, her mother wanted to teach her daughter all of the details of preparing an appropriate Christmas supper for her own husband and family someday. Maggie always bought a live turkey, butchered it, and completely prepared it herself. It was a skill she learned on the family farm in Ireland.

Helen went to the market with her mother and purchased the turkey which they carried home in a flimsy, chicken-wire cage. Once back in their apartment, Maggie took out a cutting board and a large knife and laid them both on the kitchen table as Helen stood by, hovering over the cage enclosed turkey. Maggie grabbed a sharpening stone in one hand and the large knife in the other and began sliding the knife back and forth across the stone until its edge was razor sharp.

"Helen, take the bird out of the cage. Hold it tight and keep a good grip on its wings."

Helen struggled with the turkey as it flailed about. She managed to remove it from its wired enclosure and keep it under control, holding it as firmly as she could.

"Good girl. Now bring it over to the table."

The turkey cackled wildly and thrashed its head back and forth as Helen moved closer to the kitchen table.

"Now Helen, put the bird down on the table and hold him still."

Helen leaned over, placed the gobbler firmly on the table and pressed her weight on it to keep it still. Without saying another word, Maggie reached out, grabbed the turkey's head, stretched its neck out over the cutting board and with one strong, quick wave of the knife, severed the turkey's head from its body.

The sudden stroke of the knife, the sight of the turkey's head in Maggie's hand, and the blood gushing from the turkey's neck, so stunned Helen that she screamed and dropped the turkey on the kitchen floor. To her amazement, the turkey ran a few steps before collapsing. Although a different brand of poultry, Helen learned first-hand what the phrase, *Running around like a chicken with its head cut off*, meant. For Maggie, it was just another typical day in the kitchen or on the farm. For Helen, it was an experience she hoped never to relive.

Helen wanted to do something to support her future husband and her brothers while they were away in the service. Writing letters to them was fine, but she wanted to do more. She planted some seeds in a few pots and grew geraniums. One for Raymond and one for each of her brothers. In the spring she placed them out on the fire escape and called it her Victory Garden. She tended to those plants with loving care.

Helen and her mother were fond of listening to the radio in the evening. One particular evening, she heard President Roosevelt and Secretary of the Treasury Henry Morgenthau, Jr. appeal for help to raise money for the war effort by buying or promoting the purchase of War Bonds. Although of very modest means herself, Helen invested some of what little she had in War Stamps, which could be purchased for as little as ten cents each. War Stamps could be accumulated until they equaled the minimum purchase price for an E Series savings bond, $18.[75]. War Bonds were loans to the government to help fund the costs of the war.

Helen was proud of not only her own financial contribution to the war effort, but she volunteered organizing and attending bond rallies in New York City. She was presented with a certificate from the Treasury Department of The United States on which was inscribed, *In recognition of meritorious services,* for stepping forward to work on the War Bond campaign. She took great satisfaction in her work and proudly tacked her certificate to the wall over her bed.

In late January 1943, Raymond completed his training at the West Coast Air Corps Training Center in Santa Ana and on February 7th was transferred to Ryan Field in Hemet, California, about sixty miles east of Santa Ana in the California desert. There, Raymond and the other air corps cadets received their initial round of flight training. Most of this training was conducted on the single engine PT-17 Steaman. Instead of the typical barracks arrangement to which they had become accustomed, Raymond and four other cadets shared a small bungalow on the base.

The instructors wasted no time with their cadets. The day after Raymond's arrival, he was back in the classroom at 7:00 a.m. with sessions covering a range of subjects as diverse as engine systems to chemical warfare. Three days later, he was in the air for the first time, February 10, 1943. It was exactly one year less a day after he enlisted at Dayton's Patterson Field. His first instructor, Mr. Bowen took the craft they boarded up to 2,000 feet and let Raymond take charge of the controls. With the exception of days with inclement weather, or those dominated by studies on the ground, Raymond and his fellow pilots in training flew almost every day. By the end of the month he was performing take offs and landings by himself.

March 1, 1943 was a watershed day in Raymond's flying career. He soloed for the first time taking his aircraft up for twenty-five minutes. He was thrilled. Pay call also came for the first time at Ryan Field that day. He collected $128.75. It was more money than he or anyone in his family had ever earned in one pay-day. There was someone back East who needed the money more than he did or would save it for them for their future. He purchased a money order and sent most of the money off to Helen.

Raymond fell in love with flying, but there were some stretches of time at Ryan Field that made him a little stir crazy. For one week in March of 1943, rain, wind, or both prevented him from flying. He wrote in his diary that he was, *so bored one day that I, hitched a ride on a milk truck to Hemet. Found nothing to do and came back to base to eat cookies from home.*

In mid-March Raymond and his family in Ironton got a surprise. Raymond was given permission to board an Army Air Corps flight to Dayton, Ohio. He hoped for a chance to fly to New York to see Helen, but the opportunity never arose. He hopped on a bus in Dayton and arrived home in Ironton at 4:00 a.m. on March 13th. He tried not to wake anyone, but his father heard the creaking of the floor boards of the porch as Raymond approached the front door. Startled, his father leaped out of bed. As he started down the stairs, he could see a human silhouette standing at the door in the darkness.

"Who is that?" Clarence shouted, waking his wife and daughter Ruth.

"Dad, it's me, Raymond."

"Raymond!" Ruth shouted as she jumped out of her bed, ran past her father on the stairs, and leaped into her brother's arms, hugging him with all her might.

"I have missed you so much, Raymond."

Raymond's mother and father embraced their son and tears of happiness flowed from Merle's eyes, overjoyed at seeing her son and finding him healthy and happy. There was no more sleep to be had and the Stephenson family spent the entire day catching up on each other's lives. The family reunion was short lived though, as Raymond had to board a plane back to California the following night.

As the spring of 1943 arrived, Raymond's training flights were lengthening and he was flying as long as two to three hours at a clip. Given the length of his flights and the growing complexity of the maneuvers during aerial training, the skills he needed to acquire also changed. Slow rolls, snap rolls, and other evasive maneuvering techniques that would prove invaluable in combat, were becoming a part of his flying repertoire.

The training days were longer and his occasional repose was writing letters to Helen and the chance to see a movie now and then. Movies were an interest that he and Helen shared. In some of the letters they exchanged, they lamented how they loved to be in each other's company at the movie theater. They wrote that if they were film characters themselves, their romance wouldn't be all that different, or their love for each other any less intense than Rhett Butler's for Scarlett O'Hara in *Gone with the Wind* or Ilsa Lund's for Rick Blaine in *Casablanca*.

A stark reality for Raymond was one far from the entertaining stories on the silver screen. It was summed up in one word – elimination. The ranks of the cadets were thinning out considerably as many of them could not demonstrate the temperament or talent to successfully complete the rigorous course of instruction and training to become an aviator. Some were injured or killed in accidents and crashes. Flying became more diversified, more interesting, and more challenging. Formation flying intimidated them.

Once Raymond had mastered the ability to fly single-engine aircraft, it was time for him to pack his duffel bag again. His next stop was the Army Air Force Advance Twin Engine Pilot School at Fort Sumner, New Mexico. He had to hone his skills there to prepare himself for combat in the air. Fort Sumner was in the land of high altitude plateaus and Billy the Kid. Cattle still roamed across the plains and grazed on the wild grasses in the fields surrounding Fort Sumner.

Upon his arrival, he and his fellow trainees were summoned to a meeting in order to hear a welcoming address from Commanding Officer, Colonel James H. Higgs. Colonel Higgs' objective was to impress upon these cadets the seriousness of the task which they would undertake, the importance of their missions which would follow and the unspoken vow between all of them as soldiers gathered in a common cause.

Mustering up at the Army Air Force Advance Twin Engine Pilot School, Fort Sumner, New Mexico, 1943.

"If you have any taste at all, you will find your social possibilities are meager indeed; any free time you may have will come to be a challenge to your imagination to avoid boredom and discontent. The best way to meet that challenge is to open your eyes and your heart; look at the man beside you; talk to him, learn all you can about him; make him your friend. During the combat which lies ahead of you, friendship is the one thread which will hold and sustain your faith in humanity and help you in your final readjustment for peace afterwards. For your few weeks here, make friends and keep them."

Soldiers fight for their country, but they die for their buddies.

Raymond and his counterparts took Colonel Higgs' advice to heart. In a class book that they prepared during their time at Fort Sumner, they wrote:

> *When honor, respect, and dignity fall away from the dealings among nations, harassed individuals must turn to personal attachments for a degree of faith reasonable enough to preserve their balance. Actually, friends and companions were all that meant anything real in our lives even before the days of treachery and battle. Perhaps the dark clouds of war can have their higher, brighter side.*

By the time these cadets completed their training and each received their Certificate of Proficiency from the Army Air Forces Advanced Twin Engine Pilot School on August 30, 1943, they accumulated hundreds of hours of flying time. Armament, bombardment, and advanced navigation courses rounded out their aerial menu of studies. They engaged in military training including proficiency in the use of a Colt .45 caliber pistol and the Thompson sub-machine gun. An airman never knew when he might find himself unexpectedly on the ground and in unfriendly territory. Many of these cadets were just boys when they boarded buses and trains headed to Santa Ana in December 1942. They were strangers to one another. Who were these fellows who longed to take to the skies on behalf of their families, friends, and to defend their country? They wrote again in their class book.

We left our varied families and backgrounds to share that of cadet training. Our fathers are butchers, brick masons, tax assessors, welders, lawyers and doctors. You will find them on farms, behind small grocery store counters, operating elevators in large department stores, selling insurance or real estate, inspecting army material, teaching school, running trains or building ships and airplanes. Most of our mothers are full time housewives, though some of them are nurses, clerks or business women. Some of us had more money than others; we went to different schools, lived in different states; we speak with many accents, but the thing we have in common is the greatest bond of all - we are all plain Americans, all in love with flying, all resolved to destroy the Nazism and Shintoism which threatens us.

What did we used to do? A lot of us came directly from civilian life. G class had been nearly all previous GI's, but we have a good percentage of what we old soldiers of five months call "fresh meat." Name any position you want and one of us held it or were training to do so.

We were bankers, payroll clerks, accountants and students of economics; we ran a little florist shop in the deep south, operated machines in a Middle Western factory, sold insurance in New York or Chicago; we played in small bands at night in Virginia; we operated a theatre in Miami. At Boulder Dam we drove trucks and a big crane. We drove buses; we were mechanics, machinists and railroad men. One of us tuned accordions; another was apprentice to a funeral director and embalmer. We were laborers and warehouseman; we washed dishes or waited on tables to study English literature or engineering.

Only a bare third of us have had a year or more of college work. Most of us finished high school and either studied on our own for a job or learned one as an apprentice.

Cessna AT-17/UC-78 Bobcat twin engine trainer, Army Air Force Advance Twin Engine Pilot School, Fort Sumner, New Mexico.

The ranks of cadets were pruned as the challenges of Army Air Corps pilot training grew. At Fort Sumner, the art of flying became more diversified and complex. There was just enough formation flying to intimidate cadets and yet, entice them to do more. Night flying wore them down and caused fatigue. Flying blind on instruments only, shattered some nerves. Long cross country flights played tricks with cadet's minds. Fort Sumner, this collection of dirt covered barracks in the middle of nowhere wasn't a place anyone wanted to call home.

Training didn't always go smoothly. Cadets were under a lot of pressure and were often tense and on edge. A single incident or a collection of miscues or errors could be reason enough for a cadet to be eliminated from the program. On July 6, 1943, Raymond was scheduled for a routine training flight on a twin engine Cessna AT-17/UC-78 Bobcat at 2:30 in the afternoon. Cadet Stephenson boarded the aircraft with his instructor, Second Lieutenant J.B. Latham and a second cadet, Charles D. Summers. A pre-flight inspection was completed by Corporal E.J. Sewell and Second Lieutenant Latham. Cadet Stephenson, sat in the pilot's position at the controls, with Latham seated in the co-pilot's place to Stephenson's right. Cadet Summers was sitting behind Lieutenant Latham. Stephenson received instructions to taxi to the end of runway number thirty-five. The engines were checked and Stephenson received clearance for an immediate take off. Stephenson taxied the aircraft onto the end of the runway and then gave it the gun.

The airplane sped down the runway, but before it left the ground, something went wrong. It abruptly and inexplicably turned hard to the left. Stephenson cut the throttles completely and tried to regain control of the aircraft, but to no avail. Latham took over the controls at that point and applied the right brake hard while giving the left throttle a boost. The measures he took were too late to bring the aircraft under control. The airplane continued in its hard left trajectory. A moment later the right landing gear gave way and the plane nose-dived into the runway. The craft skidded to an abrupt halt, but not before the propeller and landing gear were smashed beyond repair and the nose, fuselage and right wing were severely damaged. Although all aboard were shaken up, no one was seriously injured.

Raymond had come a long way from Ironton and worked relentlessly to get this far. Would this be the end of the line for him? Elimination from the program would have broken his spirit and crushed his dreams. The nine longest days of Raymond's life passed as the crash incident was investigated. Captain James E. Grant, the Operations Officer at Fort Sumner, reached the conclusion after reviewing all of the reports of this aircraft incident that the tail wheel locking pin of the aircraft was not in the proper position and should have been double checked. All of the steps in the pre-flight checklist had not been properly executed. Captain Grant absolved Raymond of all responsibility for the crash noting in his report that, *responsibility for the accident is instructor 100%.*

Raymond learned a valuable lesson the hard way. An entire team is responsible for getting an aircraft off the ground and safely back down again after the completion of an assignment. A simple oversight by a member of the ground crew or another flight crew member could meet with disastrous results.

Being a cadet was rugged work. Flying was tough. Ground school was arduous. The physical training may have been the toughest of all. One cadet mumbled as he dragged himself through a particularly demanding physical training session, "Are we gonna' fly 'em or carry 'em?" Many a cadet, including Raymond, looked for special strength beyond the classrooms, physical training facilities, and the experience of ascending to new heights at the controls of an aircraft. The chapel was a busy place at Fort Sumner. The chaplain was an active man, swamped by his duties as a source of comfort and strength for Raymond and many of his fellow cadets.

On August 30, 1943, Raymond no longer had to worry about being eliminated. He successfully completed and graduated from the Army Advance Twin Engine Pilot School. He received his commission as a Second Lieutenant at the commencement ceremony and proudly wore the bars of an officer on his shoulders. The chest of his uniform was adorned with the wings of an Army Air Corps pilot. Commencement ceremonies are often viewed as an ending, but for Raymond and the other young aviators in his squad, it was just the beginning.

1880's • 1890's • 1900's • 1910's • 1920's • 1930's • 1940's • 1950's

SEPTEMBER 1943

A Reunion

In my heart, I never left you.

— *Anonymous*

ate brought Helen and Raymond together for the first time fourteen months earlier in New York City's Central Park. Perhaps fate played a role again in the timing of the completion of Raymond's training at Fort Sumner. His commission as a Second Lieutenant in the Army Air Corps and his certification as a pilot were conferred upon him on August 30, 1943. The timing was perfect. He was granted a week of leave just six days before the date when his fiancée would reach her eighteenth birthday. The day that Raymond and Helen anxiously anticipated for more than a year was now quickly approaching. The day they could marry. Helen had waited patiently in New York. Her only contact with Raymond for the eleven months he was gone was through the frequent letters they exchanged.

Although Raymond had written to his parents and sisters about Helen, they still hadn't met her and both Helen and Raymond agreed that it wouldn't be appropriate for them to marry before his family could meet his fiancée. They decided to get married in Raymond's home town of Ironton. Helen's mother wanted to see her youngest daughter's wedding, but understood under the circumstances. Maggie couldn't travel to Ohio and leave Pop alone. She was reluctant to let Helen travel by herself on such a long journey and to such an unfamiliar place, so Helen's younger brother Joey would accompany her on the trip to Ohio.

Helen's father was opposed to her leaving New York regardless of the circumstances or with whom she was traveling. He hadn't met Raymond, having been hospitalized during the time of Helen and Raymond's courtship. Pop was generally quite docile, particularly after returning from treatment. However, when Maggie told him that Helen was leaving for Ohio to marry an Army Air Corps pilot, Pop went into a rage. He yelled, screamed, and cried. He was sick with worry and thought Helen was throwing her life away over an infatuation with a soldier.

"How can you let our youngest daughter run off hundreds of miles away with a stranger? She's just a child. I won't be havin' it."

"Pop, Helen is just like me. She needs to go. She must leave here, just as I left my family in Ireland to come to America to be with you."

Pop pounded his fist on the kitchen table. "It's not the same damn it!"

"Oh, isn't it now!" Maggie shouted back.

Helen went. She said goodbye to her father and little brother Johnny before she left the apartment, headed to the station to board a train to Ohio. Helen didn't own a fancy dress or gown in which to be married and had little money to purchase one. As she left the apartment she asked her mother what she should do about a wedding dress.

"Here is five dollars, Helen. It is all I have. Stop by Sally's on your way to the train station and pick out a pretty dress."

Maggie kissed her daughter on the cheek and reserved her tears until Helen was out of sight.

Pop was so upset with Helen, he wouldn't say goodbye. He watched her and Joey leave the building and walk along 47th Street from the bedroom window. Once they were out of sight, Pop went through the entire apartment looking for any photographs he could find of Helen. As he found them, he tore them into little pieces while sobbing uncontrollably. Helen doted on Pop more so than the other children. She watched over and protected him in his darkest hours.

With a dress from Sally's and a handful of items packed away in a battered, brown leather suitcase, Helen, just two days shy of her eighteenth birthday, along with her brother Joey, all of sixteen, boarded the first of a number of trains headed to Ironton. The adventure that Helen had envisioned on her first trip beyond New York City was not quite what she expected. Sixteen hours of travel in the least expensive accommodations on board the train was uncomfortable. The train was crowded. Standing room only. Helen and Joey were lucky to have gotten seats next to a window. The passenger car was hot much of the time because of the overcrowding. The heat and Helen didn't get along and she opened the window next to her and stuck her head out for a breath of fresh air. After several minutes, she pulled herself back in.

"Helen, what happened to your face?" Joey asked.

"What do you mean?"

"Your face is turning black."

"Oh dear God. What will Raymond think?"

A nearby passenger heard the exchange between Helen and Joey and interrupted.

"Miss, I wouldn't stick my head out the window. You're not turning black. The dirty, sooty steam from the coal fired engine is all over your face. It'll wash off."

Anxiously waiting at the Ironton train station were Raymond and his father. At his son's insistence, Clarence drove to the train station nearly one hour prior to the train's scheduled arrival with his nervous and restless son in tow. Raymond wanted to be absolutely certain that he was waiting at the station when the train arrived and could see its precious cargo the moment she stepped off the train.

Father and son stood together side by side on the station platform. Clarence, wearing a white collared shirt and bow tie, was a natty dresser when not in his work clothes. He wasn't sure what to expect. He knew little about Helen other than what Raymond had told him and what he confided to his sister Marjorie in his letters. In one letter that Raymond sent to her from New York, he wrote that he had met, ... *the most wonderful and the prettiest girl in New York City*. Clarence and Raymond were as close as a father and son could be since the day Raymond was born. And here he was now, standing tall in the uniform of an officer in the Army Air Corps, bearing the wings of a pilot on his chest and a Lieutenant's silver bars on his shoulders. Clarence could not have been prouder of his only son, or happier for him.

Raymond and his father were standing next to the small, simple wooden ticketing office at the station when they heard the high pitched whistle of a train in the distance. Moments later, they spotted the locomotive billowing smoke on its lumbering approach to the station. As it arrived and came to a halt, Raymond glanced left and right, not wanting to wait a second longer before setting eyes on Helen for the first time in nearly a year. His father glanced up and down the station platform, anxious to see the girl Raymond told him was, unlike any girl he ever met, and with whom he wanted to spend the rest of his life.

Raymond spotted Helen's brother Joey stepping from the train onto the station platform. Joey half turned back toward the train and extended a hand up to help his sister off the train. Raymond rushed over and lunged in between Joey and the train and as Helen's first foot was about to strike the train station platform, her face beaming, Raymond embraced her before her foot could touch the ground. Raymond felt as though he was floating above the pavement as well. They embraced with such conviction and kissed with such passion, that Joey and Raymond's father thought the love struck couple might never let each other go.

"Darling, I have missed you so much," Helen whispered in Raymond's ear.

"Helen, I missed you too, but in my heart you were always with me."

Mr. Stephenson and Joey made each other's acquaintance. The two of them then heartily cleared their throats in an attempt to get Raymond and Helen's attention. With both of them breaking out in an almost childlike laugh, Raymond apologized and introduced Helen to his father. It was a nervous moment for Helen, but more so for Raymond. There was no one who Raymond respected and admired more than his father. His father's approval of the choice of a bride would mean so much to him.

"Dad, this is Miss Helen Gregg of New York City", Raymond announced to his father. With a broad, toothy smile, Mr. Stephenson greeted Helen and gently held her right hand within both of his.

"Hello Helen," Clarence said in a soft, earnest tone. "Raymond has told me so many wonderful things about you. I am very happy to finally meet you."

The warmth and friendliness of his greeting quelled a nervousness that had built for hours during Helen's long train ride to Ohio.

"Thank you so much, Mr. Stephenson. I've looked forward to meeting you, Mrs. Stephenson and Raymond's sisters for a very long time."

He invited both Helen and Joey to stay at the Stephenson's home while in Ironton, which was a good thing. Joey barely had enough money to get back to New York City and Helen was broke after buying her train ticket to get to Ohio.

After loading up the two small suitcases that contained Helen and Joey's belongings, the four of them drove to the Stephenson's home on South Seventh Street. It was a small, modest home, but Helen admired it, as the house was larger and nicer than any place that she had ever lived. She dreamed of having her own home just like it someday. The Stephenson's home was on a small plot in the tightly knit neighborhood where Raymond spent most of his life. In the backyard was a vegetable garden. Raymond's mother had a knack for tilling the soil. It helped keep food on the Stephenson family table during hard times.

When Raymond's father pulled up to the front of his home, his wife Merle and two daughters, Marjorie and Ruth, came out onto the front porch to welcome Raymond's fiancée and her brother. Raymond and Helen stepped out of the rear seat of the car hand in hand and Raymond led Helen up the front steps to the porch.

"Mom," Raymond said proudly, "I'd like you to meet my fiancée, Miss Helen Gregg of New York City."

"Welcome to our home, Helen," Merle said. "It is so nice to finally meet you."

"I was so nervous about today Mrs. Stephenson. I am very excited to meet and get to know you and your whole family."

"Raymond," his sister Marjorie blurted out, "you weren't kidding in your letters. She is pretty."

As Helen blushed, Raymond introduced her to his sisters. After sharing just a few words with her soon to be mother-in-law, Helen noticed a resemblance between her own mother and Mrs. Stephenson. They were both strong, big boned women, with strong, calloused hands. There was little doubt in Helen's mind that the traits that both her mother and Mrs. Stephenson shared were from having labored on a farm. The two matriarchs of their respective families were also quite reserved. Perhaps from the conservative Christian roots they shared.

Marjorie and Ruth were somewhat ambivalent about the arrival of this young lady from New York City who was betrothed to their brother. The former was twenty years old and the latter, sixteen. Ruth was just a bit younger than Helen, but Helen was more like a woman and Ruth, more like a kid. Marjorie took a strong liking to Helen almost instantly. In time, they became close, more like sisters than sisters-in-law.

After settling in, Helen wanted to show Raymond's sisters the dress she had purchased for the wedding ceremony. When she pulled the dress from her suitcase, Marjorie could tell immediately that it was a somewhat worn, used dress. When new, the dress was undoubtedly white, but its now yellowed state belied the fact that the years and its lack of proper care had been unkind to its appearance.

"Helen, this is a very nice dress, but what do you think of looking at some other dresses and outfits in some of the stores downtown?"

"I like that idea, Marjorie, but I spent the last of the money I had on my train fare to get here."

"Don't worry about that, Helen. We'll figure something out."

The wedding was the following day, so Helen and Marjorie went shopping right away. They found a very smart looking, not quite white, but pale woman's suit with a button down jacket and pleated knee length skirt. Helen was excited about her new wedding attire. She had never owned such nice clothing. Marjorie also bought a beautiful corsage to be pinned to the lapel of her jacket for the wedding ceremony. Helen was so taken by her friendliness and generosity, she asked Marjorie to be her maid of honor.

The day before Helen boarded the train with Joey to make the trip out to Ohio, one of Helen's older brothers, Willie, sat her down for a talk. He knew that Helen was very naïve and had never had a serious boyfriend before meeting Raymond. It wasn't that Helen had never attracted the attention of other suitors. In fact a neighborhood friend, Jack Horosky, had asked Helen to marry him before Raymond proposed. Helen broke his heart when she told Jack, ten years older than Helen, that it was not to be.

"Jack, you are one of the nicest guys I know, but you're just too old for me."

Willie knew that in the Gregg household, like many other very reserved and conservative Irish Catholic families, matters of romance and sexuality were rarely discussed.

"What do you know about the birds and the bees, Helen?"

"Birds and bees? What are you talking about, Willie?"

Not surprisingly, Helen knew virtually nothing about what typically transpires on one's wedding night.

"The night of the day that you and Raymond get married, he is going to want to do certain things with you."

"What kinds of things?"

Willie was mortified. The Gregg women never discussed such things in detail among themselves, let alone have a conversation between the men and the women in the family about honeymoon matters.

"Um, I'm sure Raymond will know what to do and he can explain it all to you. I just want to tell you that Raymond is a good man and you can trust him to do the proper thing."

Helen was mystified by her discussion with Willie.

After her arrival in Ohio, she had a similar conversation with her soon to be mother-in-law about her wedding and the honeymoon night. Mrs. Stephenson escorted Helen to her bedroom and sat her down on the edge of the bed.

"Helen, what do you know about your wedding night?"

"My brother Willie asked me the same thing before I left home to come here. I can't say that I know anything more than before we talked. He said Raymond would know."

"I was just like you, Helen. I hadn't the foggiest notion about what happens between married men and women before Raymond's father and I got married. Did you ever talk about this with your mother?"

"No."

"These are matters that are sometimes never spoken of. Not by my mother with me and not yet by me with my own daughters. Raymond is a kind and gentle man Helen. He is just like his father. I'm sure he will be with you, in the same way my husband was with me. It will be just fine."

Helen wasn't sure what she was trying to say, but she did know that she was tiring of all of the cryptic and mysterious wedding night conversations. The more she sought answers, the more she conjured up questions. But, she knew after speaking with Willie and Raymond's mother, that whatever this was all about, it would be okay.

1880's • 1890's • 1900's • 1910's • 1920's • 1930's • 1940's • 1950's

↑

SEPTEMBER 6, 1943

The Wedding

I once dreamed of an elegant wedding.
I now wish only that he would make me his wife.
— *Anonymous*

This wasn't just the day that would join Raymond and Helen together in holy matrimony; it was also Helen's 18th birthday. Helen woke up early to the sound of a pair of cardinals chirping, nestled in the front yard willow tree as the morning sunlight pierced through a small crack between the curtains of the bedroom window. Raymond and Helen had already obtained a marriage license and had spoken to the priest at Saint Lawrence O'Toole Roman Catholic Church in Ironton about the ceremony. Helen would have loved to exchange her vows with Raymond in the beautifully ornate church on Center Street, but according to Catholic dogma at the time, Raymond, being a non-Catholic, was precluded from being married inside the church. The priest, Father William J. Reilly, agreed to marry Helen and Raymond. However, the ceremony had to take place in the parish rectory rather than in the church.

Before Helen's arrival, Raymond told his parents that he pledged to Helen's mother that they would be married by a Catholic priest. Clarence and Merle were disconcerted that the wedding wouldn't be held in their Baptist church, but their son's happiness trumped their disappointment.

Raymond and Helen with the best man and Helen's brother, Joseph Gregg and Raymond's sister and maid of honor, Marjorie Stephenson, September 6, 1943.

Raymond was rather fond of Helen's brother Joey and asked him if he would serve as his best man. Joey proudly and gratefully agreed to do so. Helen had asked Marjorie to serve as her maid of honor; however, in addition to being deprived of the opportunity to be married inside the church, Helen was denied her choice of maid of honor.

Father Reilly inquired as to the faiths of the best man and maid of honor. Marjorie, being a congregant of the First Baptist Church, was told by Father Reilly that she was ineligible to be the maid of honor and official witness to the marriage, because she wasn't Catholic. So as not to postpone the wedding ceremony that Raymond and Helen had already waited more than a year to hold, the rectory housekeeper, who happened to be cleaning the rectory at that time, stood by Helen's side during the ceremony. Helen didn't object to the housekeeper joining them, but she insisted that Marjorie join them as well. It would be unlikely to find a young woman more devoted to her faith than Helen, but even she thought it pointless to deny her a maid of honor of her own choosing, or be able to stand before the altar in a Catholic church to recite her marriage vows.

Nothing could spoil this day though. It had been fifteen months since Helen and Raymond first set eyes upon each other in New York's Central Park and fell passionately in love. More than one year went by since their engagement waiting for Helen's eighteenth birthday to arrive so that they could be joined together forever. With Raymond's mother and father present, as well as his two sisters and his Uncle Kent and Aunt Dorothy, Raymond recited his vows to love and cherish Helen for all time, as Helen's brother Joey stood proudly at his side. Helen trembled with excitement as she next declared her undying devotion for Raymond, while he enveloped her petit hands in his. They gently slipped simple silver bands over each other's ring fingers.

"With this ring I wed thee."

It was the most beautiful and exciting moment of Helen's life.

There was no fancy reception after the small, intimate ceremony where Helen and Raymond pledged to love and treasure one another for eternity. Conservative Baptist families weren't much for parties and dancing. The family returned to the Stephenson's home where Merle, Marjorie, and Ruth prepared a nice supper for everyone. The cake that followed the meal served a dual purpose. It was consumed first and foremost in celebration of the marriage between Raymond and Helen, but it also commemorated Helen's eighteenth birthday.

The newly united couple spent their honeymoon night at the Stephenson's home. Helen was nervous about her wedding night. Not only because of the shroud of mystery over the occurrences of a wedding night, but because her new mother-in-law and father-in-law were in an adjoining bedroom.

Raymond and Helen on their wedding day and Helen's 18th birthday, Ironton, Ohio, September 6, 1943.

Helen and Raymond were virgins. He knew more than Helen though. Raymond was patient and understanding. He was kind and gentle, knowing that this was Helen's first time. She knew so little about the physical relationship between men and women. She was apprehensive, but never frightened. She could never be scared in Raymond's arms. Ever so gently, Helen and Raymond consummated their vows and love for each other that night in marital embrace.

The next morning brought a second round of nervousness when Helen awoke.

"Raymond. Oh my gosh. What if your mother and father heard us last night?"

"I'm sure they were sound asleep by then, darling."

There was an unusual silence at the kitchen table that morning as everyone gathered for breakfast. No one mustered much more than a "good morning" to one another. As they ate the eggs that Merle had prepared and drank coffee, Raymond looked up at Helen and chuckled. Helen giggled. Mr. and Mrs. Stephenson looked up from their plates over the tops of their spectacles and grinned.

"What's so funny?" Raymond's youngest sister asked.

Raymond burst out laughing.

"Aw nothing, you just wouldn't understand."

After breakfast, Raymond excused himself, kissed Helen on the cheek, and told her he had to run a few errands, but wouldn't be gone long. Raymond had to leave Ohio the next day for his next assignment. His destination was the Roswell Army Airfield in Roswell, New Mexico. Raymond had no idea how long it might be until he returned to his hometown, so he wanted to see a few people, perhaps for the last time, before he left.

As Raymond headed out the front door of his parent's home dressed in his uniform, his father followed him out onto the front porch.

"Hold on a second, Raymond," Clarence called to his son. "There's something I need to tell you before you run off."

Raymond turned back toward the house, facing his father and asked, "Sure, Dad, what's that?"

"Although your mother and me only just met Helen and haven't had a whole lot of time to get to know her better, we like her just fine. Your sisters like her too."

"Thank you, Dad," Raymond responded as he placed a hand on his father's shoulder. "That means a lot to me and it will to Helen too. She was pretty nervous about meeting everyone and worried you might not like her being from New York City and Catholic and all."

"And one other thing, Raymond, after you leave us tomorrow, make sure you write to your mother often. She misses you and worries about you. She's had a tearful night or two while you've been away."

"Gee Dad, Mom's never said anything to me about that."

Clarence shrugged his shoulders and shook his head. "Naw, your mom never would. It's not her way."

"I'll try to write every week, Dad. Tell Mom not to worry.

Me and Helen will be just fine."

And with that, Raymond stepped forward, gave his father a hug and went off about his business.

At the top of Raymond's visit list was his best boyhood friend and cousin, Jack Bradshaw. Jack had joined the United States Navy and had coincidentally run into Raymond when they were both stationed in California. As kids, they spent countless hours swimming in the creek that flowed through the Bradshaw farm. After cooling off on a hot summer day they would sit by the edge of the creek in the sun and muse about what their futures would hold. To a great extent, many of Raymond's expectations in adulthood had already been realized. He dreamed of becoming a pilot. He talked about how one day he would travel far outside the borders of Ohio. But most importantly, he had just married a girl of whom he never specifically dreamed, but who now made every other dream he ever had seem less important.

Another of Raymond's visits on this, his last day in Ironton before shipping out, was to the offices of The Tribune. The last civilian job Raymond held before enlisting in the Army Air Corps was as an employee in the newspaper's circulation department. He had a long relationship with The Tribune, having worked there for many years delivering newspapers as a boy on his bicycle. Raymond was well regarded by everyone at the newspaper and fair to say, he was held in high esteem by everyone in Ironton who knew him. After visiting for a bit with his former colleagues at the newspaper, he bid them goodbye and they in turn wished him well. Later that day, C.J. McCarthy, a columnist for The Tribune, took to his typewriter and in the newspaper's About Town column, McCarthy wrote the following:

They leave boys and come back men. A few years ago Raymond Stephenson, son of Mr. and Mrs. Clarence R. Stephenson of 2010 South Seventh Street came to The Tribune as a carrier boy. Later on he graduated from high school and was employed in the circulation department of the paper. He was a quiet and unassuming lad and save for the fact that he did his work well you hardly knew he was around. Then, some two years ago, Raymond joined the army and became part of the nation's aerial ground forces. This week he dropped in at The Tribune office and on his collar were the gold bars of a lieutenant and on his sleeve the wings of the air corps. He had been commissioned as a pilot and had been recommended for the pilot place on one of the big B-17's. No doubt he'll make good therein the same quiet way he made good at home. In the past couple of years boys you know drop out of your life. They disappear and sort of subconsciously you know they are in the armed forces. Then, one day they come back men and you wonder if they can be the same boys you knew. You wonder because you knew them as immature youths, little concerned with the battle of life. Well, they're back. With calm self-assurance and quiet determination.

1880's • 1890's • 1900's • 1910's • 1920's • 1930's • 1940's • 1950's

↑

SEPTEMBER 1943

The City Girl Heads West

All journeys have destinations
of which the traveler is unaware.
— Martin Buber

After his marriage to Helen, Raymond continued with the next phase of his training as an Army Air Corps aviator at the Roswell Army Air Field in Roswell, New Mexico. Here at the Air Corps Advanced Flying School, pilots and crews conducted training missions with live bombs to make certain that pilots and bombardiers were ready for combat.

Before going live, they flew used AT-11 Beechcraft bombing trainers outfitted with one hundred pound practice bombs filled with sand, water, or a combination of the two. To measure the accuracy of the bombardiers, the practice bombs were also filled with spotting charges that created black smoke. Its impact and detonation caused a splatter effect in which the bomb casing ruptured and the sand filler served as a location indicator. For night bombing, signal cartridges that produced a flash of light and a white puff of smoke were used.

Raymond had crisscrossed the country from Ohio to New York to California and now to New Mexico a second time, to prepare him for what soon would come. Because of the distances involved and the demanding schedules, it didn't make sense for Helen to visit Raymond during the initial phases of his training. Helen and Raymond had spent enough time apart during their engagement. Now married, they agreed Helen should follow Raymond to New Mexico. However, spouses were not permitted to travel on military aircraft with their husbands.

Raymond flew to the Roswell Army Air Field, but Helen had to board a combination of buses and trains to travel there from Ironton. The newlyweds were completely and passionately in love. No amount of time on a bus or train seemed too long, or overly inconvenient, to keep Helen from being with her husband.

Even for the two days between Raymond's departure and the day that Helen boarded a bus out of Ironton, she was lonely. The day after the wedding, Helen's brother Joey left to return to New York City while Helen remained in Ohio with Raymond's family. Despite the good company of the Stephensons and the close relationship she had forged with Marjorie, Helen was anxious to join Raymond, no matter how long or how far she had to travel. Helen not only longed to be with her new husband, but she also missed her mother and siblings in New York.

It took almost three full days for Helen to travel from Ironton to Roswell. She had no sleeping accommodations on the buses or trains. Trains traveling through the south were mostly older, coal burning or oil burning steam engines. The trains could be cold, especially at night, if you were not seated close to the pot belly stove that served as the only source of heat in the passenger cars. The trains were crowded with soldiers and sailors during the war and often had standing room only. Soldiers were courteous and most often offered a seat to a woman.

The trains were equipped with a dining car that could seat up to forty people, but trying to get to the dining car through a packed train, with people often sleeping on the floor or the vestibule of the passenger cars, was a challenge. If you made it to the dining car, you could expect a significant wait to be seated or served. If you were patient though and stayed put in your seat, a porter would eventually make his way through the passenger cars and sell sandwiches and small bottles of milk. Porters also had candy such as Baby Ruth and Hershey chocolate bars to sell.

Helen was fascinated by the scenery she spied through the window of the train as it rolled and rattled along the tracks. The desert landscape of the southwest was a sight she had never experienced before. The row houses and skyscrapers of Manhattan were replaced by towering mountains. Concrete sidewalks and cobblestone streets gave way to farm fields and sand filled landscapes of prickly plants. There were more cows and horses than people in some places. As enchanted as she was with those scenes, she was disturbed by the sight of trackside shanty towns in the south. Populated mostly with colored people, she was very troubled by the deplorable conditions in which these poor souls lived. It gave her a new found appreciation for the neighborhood in which she grew up.

Office of Defense Transportation's troops on the move awareness poster.

Some folks on the trains found it easy to sleep, even though they would go hours and days seated in an upright position. The clickety-clack of the train rolling across the tracks produced a sleep inducing cadence for some passengers. Not for Helen, however. She was only eighteen years old and had never traveled alone anywhere beyond New York City. She dozed off from time to time, but she could never get all that comfortable. She was fearful of missing a stop to switch trains, or bypassing her final destination. The conductors on the train were helpful and courteous, but if they were especially busy, they might forget to alert a passenger that his or her stop was just ahead. If you slept through it, the time and distance devoted to a return trip could be lengthy.

In spite of the rigors of travel, Raymond's eighteen year old bride vowed that not only would she make her own way out

Helen sporting Raymond's cap and wings, Roswell Army Air Field, Roswell, New Mexico, October 3, 1943.

west to New Mexico to be with her husband, but she was determined that no matter where he went until being assigned to duty in the war, she would be by his side.

Having been promoted to the rank of 2nd Lieutenant and received his Silver Wings after completing the most recent phase of his training, Raymond was able to acquire the use of separate housing for he and Helen. The quarters consisted of a small cabin with an outhouse. Considering the conditions in which she was raised,

Helen liked it just fine. Even though she and Raymond didn't own it, Helen embraced it as their first home as husband and wife.

Helen was content in their little cabin. She marveled at the view of the desert and the surrounding mountains of New Mexico, particularly at sunset when red, orange, and yellow hues were created by the sunlight reflecting off the mountainsides, as the sun settled on the western horizon. In the evening, she and Raymond sat side by side and arm in arm on the front steps of their cabin watching the natural light show, so grateful to be with one another. Sometimes they'd sit there into the evening when the desert sky exchanged the reddish-yellow illumination of the sun for the heavenly glow of the stars. The rural, southwestern sky, with its absence of artificial light, revealed thousands of stars that were never visible in the incandescent lit skies above New York City. Raymond pointed out and described dozens of celestial formations and the constellations that he learned to identify as a boy scout. They talked about having children one day and eventually settling down in their own home after Raymond fulfilled his military commitment.

Helen's loneliness dissipated as she now had Raymond's company each day after his training sessions were complete. She also began to meet some of the wives of the other officers. All of them were older than Helen. Most of them were better educated and worldlier than she, which initially made her uncomfortable. Many of them had been army wives longer, or were more experienced in the ways of the world in general and the practices of military life in particular.

One evening Helen and Raymond were invited by a senior officer to be the guests of him and his wife at the officer's club.

Upon their arrival, the senior officer asked his guests if they would like a drink before dinner.

"How about you, Helen? What kind of cocktail would you like?"

Helen wasn't a drinker. She never had an alcoholic drink before and could not think of the name of a particular cocktail to order. She paused for a moment. She didn't want to look like some country bumpkin or dopey kid who doesn't know anything about socializing. She glanced toward the bartender and said the first thing that popped into her head.

"Yes, I'd love to have a cocktail, thank you. I'll have a shrimp cocktail."

"Are you sure that's what you want, Ma'am?" Asked the bartender.

"Oh, absolutely. That's exactly what I would like."

The others ordered their drinks, which were served quite promptly. Helen sat and wondered why her cocktail was taking so much longer to prepare than all of the other drinks. A few more minutes lapsed and a waiter placed a shrimp cocktail before her. Helen had never seen one before. She leaned over and whispered in Raymond's ear.

"How am I supposed to drink this thing?"

Helen struggled at first fitting in with the other women in and around Roswell Army Air Field. She still had a bit of tomboy in her from her hardscrabble days in Hell's Kitchen. The other wives seemed overly concerned with matters of a more genteel nature or their status on the base. Helen grew particularly close with one of the other young wives though. Her name was Maureen. She was a meek and shy woman from a small town in Nebraska. Like Helen, she wasn't the typical officer's wife. She didn't understand the military wife protocol. She was the nicest person Helen met during her time at the base.

Helen's base entry permit, Roswell Army Air Field.

One afternoon, while their husbands were on duty, Helen, her friend Maureen and a handful of other women gathered at the officers club to visit. As the afternoon and their conversations went on and they enjoyed some iced tea, one of the women began needling Maureen with condescending and insulting remarks about her hillbilly accent and unfashionable dress. Helen watched and listened for a while until the point at which her young friend was close to tears.

"Knock it off," Helen told the berating woman.

The woman dismissed Helen with the same insensitivity she had shown to Maureen and went on with her degrading remarks.

"I'm telling you," Helen warned her again, "you better knock it off."

"And what if I don't?" The callous woman challenged.

That was all Helen needed to hear. She got up from her chair and walked across the room toward the woman. As Helen approached her, the shrew rose from her chair. The woman was a head taller than Helen and bigger boned. Helen confronted her again.

"Apologize to Maureen."

The woman placed the index finger of her right hand on the center of Helen's chest and gave her a shove.

"I'm not apologizing to anyone."

Helen reared back with her right fist and landed a haymaker square on the woman's jaw, knocking her to the ground. The other women gasped and sat in stunned silence. For good measure, Helen sat on the aggressor, now turned victim. Helen grabbed her wrists and pinned her down.

"You tell Maureen you're sorry and I'll let you up."

The other women were aghast and just watched, frozen in place. The woman struggled to break free, but Helen had her securely pinned to the floor.

"Let me up, you little bitch!"

"I didn't hear you say you're sorry."

"Fine. I'm sorry," the woman said half-heartedly.

Helen got up and helped the frazzled and disheveled woman to her feet. Without saying another word, Helen walked away with Maureen in tow.

Later that day, Raymond arrived at their quarters as Helen was in the kitchen preparing dinner.

"Helen, we need to talk."

"Oh Raymond, you're home. How was your day?"

"Please tell me it isn't true."

Helen feigned ignorance.

"Is what not true, Raymond?"

"Please tell me that you didn't actually hit a captain's wife today."

"I can tell you that, but it would be a lie. I didn't know she was a captain's wife. If I knew the battleaxe was a captain's wife I probably wouldn't have punched her and I definitely wouldn't have sat on her."

"You sat on her too?"

Helen started to cry. She feared that her rash behavior may have jeopardized Raymond's standing and future in the

Air Corps. She would never intentionally do anything to hurt, embarrass or upset him. Raymond gave her a hug.

"It's okay darling. Some of the other women who were there said that the captain's wife definitely stepped over the line. Even she realizes that she took things too far with Maureen. You were just trying to defend your friend and to be honest, I admire that. But, nothing like this can ever happen again."

"It never will," Helen demurely responded. "I promise."

Raymond continued his service in New Mexico and was selected for the B-17 pilot training program. The B-17, the Army Air Forces' Flying Fortress, was a mainstay heavy bomber used by the United States Army Air Forces in World War II. It was used principally by the Eighth Air Force, based in the United Kingdom, where it made its wartime debut in 1942. It was a very formidable adversary against the Nazis in the skies over Europe.

When he completed this phase of his training at Roswell Army Air Field, Raymond was transferred to Hill Field, approximately thirty miles north of Salt Lake City, Utah near Ogden. Hill Air Field was named after Major Ployer Peter Hill who died as the result of injuries he sustained from the crash of a Boeing Model 299, which was the prototype for the B-17. It was in Utah that Raymond would receive his crew assignment.

Helen wanted to follow Raymond to his newest destination and he wanted her by his side, so it was time to board a bus again. Most of her interstate bus rides were boring and exhausting. The bus trip from New Mexico to her destination in Utah was two days long and nearly a thousand miles.

Toward the end of one long day aboard the bus, the second of her trip, it drove through a mountainous highway pass near Park City, Utah. As though out of nowhere, snow and wind, the likes of which Helen had never seen or could have imagined, descended upon the bus as it barreled down along the two lane highway that winded snake-like from Park City toward Salt Lake City. The driver struggled to control the bus. He couldn't slow it down or stop it because the roads were treacherously slick. Nor could he see well. The intensity of the snow fall and the howling, swirling winds, diminished visibility to only a few feet. The driver narrowly avoided hitting another bus that had flipped over on its side along the edge of the pavement.

Helen was terrified as the bus swerved across the slippery lanes of the highway. Images of Raymond, her mother, Pop, and her brothers and sisters raced through her mind. Would she ever see them again?

"God be with me. God bless me. God save me. God be with me. God bless me. God save me." She recited it over and over again as her mother taught her when she was a little girl.

Other passengers prayed, some screamed, and others sat silently as they grasped the arm rests, the seat in front of them, or the passenger next to them, with white knuckled fists. As Helen prayed, the road began to level off and straighten. The bus continued to fish tail, but now not quite as severely. Helen's prayers were finally answered as the bus driver managed to bring the bus under control.

Helen felt squeamish at this point. She didn't know if it was something she had eaten or if the uneasiness in her stomach was caused by the swerving and speed of the bus. It might have been brought on by the fear that embraced her as the bus plummeted down the mountain highway. She was sick to her stomach. She never felt so nauseous before. She burst out of her seat and ran to the front of the bus.

"Please, please stop and let me out. I'm sick."

The driver pulled off to the side of the road and opened the door. Helen leaped off the steps into knee deep snow. Chilled by blustery winds, she bent over and vomited violently, over and over again.

1880's • 1890's • 1900's • 1910's • 1920's • 1930's • 1940's • 1950's

↑

NOVEMBER 1943

A Crew Comes Together

Coming together is a beginning.
Keeping together is progress.
Working together is success.

—*Henry Ford*

Hill Air Field near Ogden Utah was a long way from home for most of the soldiers stationed there. They were far from the places they grew up and many miles from family and friends. Their only link to home and the world outside the armed forces was an occasional letter. It was here that Raymond learned who the members of a new family of sorts would be. Brothers in the United States Army Air Forces were teamed together into flight crews. They spent the hours and days together. Their lives were held in each other's hands.

Raymond Stephenson, pilot and flight commander, was a leader of such a crew. A pretty tall order for a twenty-three year old, small town boy from Ohio to handle. Although a number of names and faces came and went throughout Raymond's time as a flight commander, a core crew was assembled that shared almost all of their missions together. Co-pilot duties were assigned to Second Lieutenant Joseph Ward from Bloomfield, New Jersey. The crew's navigator, Second Lieutenant Eugene W. Swiatnicki, was from Chicago, Illinois. Oakland, California was home to the flight engineer, Sergeant Earl N. Westerholm. Sergeant Joseph C. Minery, who hailed from Meriden, Connecticut, was their Flying Fortress radio operator. Rome, New York was home to ball turret gunner Sergeant Leonard L. Licurse and gunner, Sergeant Keith J. Clinton, a native son of Grand Rapids, Michigan rounded out the nucleus of their team.

Their story is no great war saga. Such was the case for most of the airmen. They put on their uniforms each day and quietly, bravely, and effectively carried out their duty. Theirs was a story with an uncomplicated plot summarized in four words; war, duty, friendship, and flying. They tried to live by the words of their former commanding officer, Colonel Higgs.

The best way to meet your challenge is to open your eyes and heart. Look at the man beside you. Talk to him; learn all you can about him; make him your friend. During the combat which lies ahead of you, friendship is the one thread which will hold you and sustain your faith in humanity and help you in your final readjustment for peace afterwards.

Raymond in his pilot attire, 1944.

Every cadre of young men, whether housed in a college dormitory, sharing a locker room, or assigned as a crew to combat an enemy from the skies in a B-17, has as many personalities as it has members. Raymond was a quiet, straight laced young leader.

He never smoked cigarettes or drank alcoholic beverages and he never cussed. However, it was a mistake to interpret his quiet demeanor as a sign of weakness. Beneath his gentle façade was a firm and fearless soldier and leader. As a pilot and flight commander, he demanded discipline and loyalty of himself and expected no less from his crew. He was tough with the men under his command when he had to be. He treated them with respect and they respected him in kind.

Flight engineer Earl Westerholm was a gregarious young man and a dead serious crew member when it came to fulfilling his duties. The flight engineer, along with the pilot, typically checked out the aircraft completely during pre-flight inspection. Earl knew the technical specifications of the B-17 inside and out and could deal with electrical or mechanical problems whether on the ground or while in flight. He oversaw the enlisted men on the crew and it was also his responsibility to make sure the aircraft was fueled properly and adequately equipped. He spent six months of full-time training to become a certified flight engineer at the Amarillo, Texas Flight Engineering School. Earl also completed the gunner's school in Las Vegas, Nevada. The top turret guns were his responsibility during combat. From the time of a pre-mission briefing until the crew's safe return back to their base and the post-mission de-briefing, Earl was all business.

Joe Ward and Lenny Licurse were cut from the same piece of timber. They were both outgoing, with big personalities. Although both of them were very dedicated soldiers and extremely adept at their respective roles on the crew, they considered it no crime or dereliction of their responsibilities to have a little fun when they were off duty. They were young, confident, handsome, and single. They were the ladies men.

The crew had the luxury of a young woman on the base who laundered their uniforms. On laundry days, Lenny always cheerfully volunteered to bring the laundry for the entire crew to the young woman who washed, pressed, and folded their uniforms. The rest of the crew detected a pattern and noticed that Lenny was always gone for several hours and returned to the barracks a bit disheveled. There was a lot more than the washing and pressing of uniforms getting done on laundry days they figured.

Joe Minery was the diminutive one of the bunch. He was all of five foot four and weighed one hundred and thirty pounds. He had a great sense of humor and was a lot of fun to be around. Joe loved olives and couldn't get enough of them. He coaxed his crewmates to create diversions in the mess hall so that he could sneak into the kitchen and swipe a jar.

Navigator Eugene Swiatnicki was recognized as one of the best at his trade. His ability to direct a flight and be spot on with establishing direction and location was uncanny. If he estimated a time of arrival at a target or destination, it was rarely just an estimate, but rather, an accurate prediction. He was a master of the four methods of navigation employed at the time on their B-17 - pilotage, dead reckoning, radio, and celestial.

Keith Clinton was a happy go lucky guy of good Christian upbringing. His crewmates respected him for his skills as a gunner. His deep faith and maturity were matched only by his courage. The tall, strapping lad didn't easily squeeze into a gun turret. He loved playing cards with the other fellows on the crew and became fond of bicycle riding around the base during his sparse amount of down time.

This crew and all of their contemporaries in the Army Air Forces, came from all walks of life and from across the United

States. They left their homes, families and loved ones behind. But, here in Utah, where none of them ever imagined they'd find themselves, they were bound together on a mission to stop a common enemy.

The wives of those who were married remained at home, some caring for their sons and daughters. For those with extended families with which they could stay, there was comfort. Others were isolated and alone. Theirs was a heavy emotional load to carry; the loneliness of a half empty bed and the thought that the next letter, telegram, or knock on the door could be the last bit of news that they would ever hear about the man they loved.

Much to her dismay, Helen learned that her husband and his crew were being relocated again. They were headed to Louisiana for the last phase of their preparation for combat duty in Europe. Helen faced more trains and buses moving her across the country, traveling alone. She survived the frightful experience of driving through a harrowing snow-storm on a mountain pass in Utah. Now, just three days after her arrival there, it was time to pack up and ride the rails and roads across America again, this time to Louisiana.

1880's • 1890's • 1900's • 1910's • 1920's • 1930's • 1940's • 1950's

NOVEMBER 1943

The Kind and the Intolerant

Our true nationality is mankind.

—H.G. Wells

Helen began a monotonous two thousand miles worth of train and bus rides from Ogden, Utah to Alexandria, Louisiana. Although some of the scenery, especially the desert and the mountains of the west, provided some distraction during her long trip east, the circuitous route she took getting to Louisiana by way of Chicago, was much more travel time than she anticipated. For hours upon hours she tried to make herself comfortable, but with limited success. During the war most trains were packed with soldiers. Railroad tracks crisscrossed the country extending from the largest cities through the most desolate regions and to many small towns. As the conflict wore on, the troops going off to war were often replaced on the trains by wounded and disfigured soldiers on their way home. Too many boys made the train ride back to their families and home towns in wooden boxes with flags draped over them.

What little sleep Helen got on the train wasn't sound or comfortable. What little she ate, was only what was available on the train from a porter hawking sandwiches as he passed through the aisles, or the ill tasting meals obtainable at a bus station. She sampled some soup on the train once, but trying to connect the small soup spoon to her mouth while the train rocked and rumbled, resulted in more soup being worn than eaten. Nothing she ate seemed to agree with her anyway and occasional spells of acute and intense nausea plagued her.

Helen had to spend money cautiously. There was only so much she could afford while making her way around the country. She generally found people to be friendly and helpful, especially when she told them about her recent marriage to a soldier and the reason for her excursions. It helped to pass the time during the hours and days of travel to chat with fellow passengers, especially a soldier with whom she might share a seat, or who sat next to her on the floor of the train.

Two days after her departure from Utah, Helen arrived in Chicago where she planned to catch a train headed south to Louisiana. Just prior to her arrival in Chicago, Helen was speaking with a conductor on the train who advised her under no uncertain terms, not to leave the train station. The streets of Chicago were no place for an unescorted young lady. Helen had no reason to leave the station, since she would only be there long enough to catch her next train.

When Helen arrived in Chicago, she went directly to the ticket window and asked for a ticket for the next leg of her trip.

"I'm sorry, miss. Because of overcrowding, the only people we can allow on that train headed for Louisiana are uniformed soldiers and wives accompanying them. If you find a hotel for the night, we might be able to get you on a train tomorrow."

Helen was going to burst into tears. Her reunion with Raymond would be delayed at least one more day. She had no extra money for a hotel and was afraid to leave the train station in any case. A soldier standing behind her overheard the conversation, approached Helen and grabbed the suitcase from her hand.

"Sweetheart, I have been looking all over for you. C'mon, before we miss our train."

Helen was puzzled initially, but she caught a wink of the soldier's eye.

"I'll be with you in a moment, darling. I just need to pay for my ticket."

Helen bought her ticket, and then she and the soldier walked away from the ticket window, out of listening distance from the clerk.

"I'm on my way to Alexandria to join my husband. He's an army pilot. I don't know what I would have done if you didn't help me."

"It's no trouble, ma'am. I'd hope that if my wife was in a fix like that, someone would help her just the same."

"I can't thank you enough."

"You're welcome. Now, let's get on that train. There's a fly boy in Louisiana who I'd imagine is mighty anxious to see you."

Helen rode the rails all the way to Shreveport, Louisiana. The rest of the trip to Alexandria and on to the nearby army air base, meant more miles on buses. Helen had little sense of the geography of the state of Louisiana, but reveled in the belief that she must not be all that far away from her destination once the train pulled into Shreveport. Helen was able to grab a quick bite to eat at a diner near the bus station before boarding the bus in Shreveport, headed toward the second to last stop remaining in her journey to join Raymond.

Helen boarded the bus slid into a seat near the front, moving to her right until she was at the window. Another young woman boarded the bus and asked if she could share the seat with Helen. Helen gladly agreed, hoping to have some company for the trip. Her new acquaintance sat down beside her next to the aisle.

"Hi. I'm Helen Gregg… uh, I mean Stephenson. Helen Stephenson. My husband's an army pilot and was just transferred from Utah to Alexandria. I'm on my way to join him."

Her young companion, a thin, pretty girl with short cropped, jet black hair, spoke with the apparent drawl of a southerner.

"Nice to meet you, Helen. I'm Loretta. I live in Kentucky, but I'm on my way back home to Red Chute, Louisiana to pay a visit with my family."

No sooner had they exchanged names, when an angry voice boomed from the front of the bus.

"Not there!"

Loretta and Helen looked up. The bus driver was staring directly at them.

A segregated bus station and a sign commonly posted in southern buses, 1940s.

Helen was startled. "I'm sorry, sir, but I don't know what you mean by, not there."

"I'm not talking to you, I'm talking to her!" the driver bellowed, as he pointed at Loretta. "We don't allow coloreds to ride in the front of the bus!"

Helen was rattled and perplexed. She rode the trolley, bus, and subway in New York City with colored people. Besides, while Loretta had a complexion darker than her, she wasn't as dark as most Negroes.

"She's not even colored," Helen said to the driver.

"I don't even let white niggers ride in the front of my bus. Now, get in the back."

Helen never heard the term before.

"What is he talking about, Loretta?"

"My daddy's white and my momma's colored. It's alright, Helen. I'll be fine. The back of the bus will get me where I need to go. It's best not to make a fuss about it."

With that, Loretta stood up and moved to the back of the bus.

Helen was angry. In her neighborhood back home it was mostly Irish, but someone from about every corner of the world either lived or worked somewhere nearby. She resented when one of her own kind was mistreated because of a brogue or their Irish heritage. She had no tolerance for bigotry, whether it was because of where someone was from, the color of their skin, or the way they spoke.

Several hours out of Shreveport, another bus transfer took place and thankfully, it was the last bus on Helen's journey to be reunited with her husband. Just a few hours after boarding this final conveyance, Helen's bus approached a roadside bus stop a few miles from her final destination. The sky was violent and the wind blustery. Sheets of rain furiously fell from the clouds. The precipitation pelted the bus so powerfully, a sharp pinging sound emanated from the surface of the bus as each drop struck its metal roof. Claps of thunder cannonaded and bolts of lightning illuminated the night sky and roadside.

As the bus slowed to a halt, Helen looked out her window. She spotted two people standing at the bus stop. One was a soldier in uniform and the other, a neatly attired woman in a tan gabardine trench coat, standing beside him. The rain was coming down like God had opened up the heavens and released a torrent of water. Helen sympathized with the two prospective passengers standing near the curb, anxiously anticipating an escape from the night's misery.

The driver opened the bus door and the soldier allowed the woman to board first. After she paid her fare and moved toward a vacant seat, the young soldier set his left boot onto the first step of the bus. The driver held up a hand.

"Where do you think you're going?"

"Uh, I'm headed back to base," the soldier politely replied.

"No niggers are allowed on this bus," the driver snapped back.

The soldier stood momentarily with one foot still on the bottom step of the bus. The next words unexpectedly came from Helen's mouth as the other passengers sat tensely and silently.

"He's a soldier at that base, just like my husband for God's sake. Let him on the bus."

Instantly the driver's venomous attack turned toward Helen.

"If you don't sit there and shut the hell up, you'll get thrown off this bus too and you can stand in the rain with the nigger."

The soldier, who looked no older than her Raymond, turned to Helen.

"Ma'am, it's alright."

"No. It's not alright."

"Ma'am, there'll be another bus along before too long. I'm sure your husband is eager to see you. Y'all stay on this bus and be on your way."

The soldier stepped back into the darkness and the drenching rainfall. The door closed and the bus pulled away. Helen gazed out the window of the bus, focused on the soldier standing in the dark. She was overcome with anger and sorrow. She prayed for the abandoned soldier as she quietly released tears.

1880's • 1890's • 1900's • 1910's • 1920's • 1930's • 1940's • 1950's

DECEMBER 1943-MARCH 1944

Lousyana

Shacks, rats, and chickens.

Helen finally reached the Alexandria Army Air Base on December 2, 1943. Raymond arrived there three days earlier. He greeted Helen with an ear to ear smile, an impassioned kiss, and a long embrace. He missed Helen intensely during her journey to join him.

"Darling, I missed you only once while we were apart. It was from the moment I took off from Utah, until this very instant."

Helen was happy to hear that Raymond secured a home for their use on the base. At least she was happy until she saw the place. Helen never imagined that she would see a home worse than the apartments in which she had lived in New York City or the Spartan housing that she and Raymond occupied in New Mexico. The shack to which they were assigned in Louisiana was deplorable. It was run down and dirty. A film of dust covered the floors and the kitchen counters. The cabinets were slick and smelled of decaying grease. The porcelain kitchen sink was cracked and stained. Except for a small wood stove, it was unheated. The hovel was so old and creaked so badly, Helen feared a stiff wind might cause it to collapse. To relieve oneself, a stroll to the outhouse in the back yard was necessary.

As always, Helen made the best of it. After her long bus trip, she was anxious to relieve herself and made her first visit to the outhouse. It wasn't much, even for an outhouse. Just a one holer. The smell inside was obnoxious, bordering on sickening. She couldn't see too well because there was no moon cut-out in the door and just a bit of light peeked through the cracks in the wall boards. An old Sears shopping catalogue sat on the floor for doing the paper work after her business was done. Helen tried to hold her breath as she lowered her undergarments and hoisted her skirt to sit down. As she lowered herself to be seated, a chicken stuck its head up through the hole, cackled wildly and scared Helen half to death. She let out a scream and Raymond came running out the screen door on the back of the shack.

Helen at the Alexandria Army Air Base, Alexandria, Louisiana, January 1944.

"Are you okay in there?" He called out to Helen.

"Yes, I'm fine," she shouted back. "You're lucky that I love you and there is a chicken that's lucky she won't be tonight's supper."

As was the case in New Mexico and Utah, Raymond was constantly busy throughout each day. Now in the company of the crew with whom he would train on the B-17 together and ultimately be assigned overseas, there was precious little time for anything unrelated to combat flight preparation. While Raymond was occupied with training, Helen did her best to make their home as clean and comfortable as possible. She scrubbed every floor, wall, cupboard, and counter-top until they were spotless.

Helen picked up groceries on her second day there. The wife of another officer on the base advised Helen to keep all of her food in the refrigerator because mice or rats would get at it no matter what drawers or cabinets she might store them in. There were many items that Helen didn't mind putting in the refrigerator, but some food just didn't taste right cold. She didn't completely disregard the warning she had gotten, so she hammered a nail into one of the walls and hung some food in a bag on it, assuming it would be safe from rodents and roaches.

After she and Raymond went to bed that evening, they both heard a scratching noise on the walls of the kitchen. It reminded Helen of the sound that her father made when he struck matches on the bedroom walls to light his pipe. When Helen got up the next morning, she saw that rats or mice had gotten to the bag of food that she hung on the nail in the kitchen wall. Between the rats, mice, bugs, humidity, outhouse stink and her bus rides coming to this place, Helen was less than enchanted with Louisiana. She also knew that at this location she would have to say her final goodbye to Raymond when he and his crew were assigned to combat. From that day forward she referred to this state as "Lousyana."

Raymond was enamored with his new duty station. In 1939, city officials in Alexandria recognized a need for a municipal airport to handle commercial air traffic and created the Alexandria Municipal Airport. As the conflict grew and spread, the City of Alexandria leased its airport

Raymond and Helen's quarters, Alexandria Army Air Base, 1944.

to the United Sates Army Air Corps for one dollar a year. On October 21, 1942 the Alexandria Army Air Base opened for operation. The base became a center for the training of crews of Boeing's B-17. Raymond found the continuous action and activity surrounding the base exhilarating. His new base was the epicenter for B-17 long range bomber training and he was in awe of the aircraft under his command.

In July 1935, an airplane unlike anyone had ever seen rolled out of a hangar at the Boeing manufacturing facility in Seattle, Washington. It had a 105 foot wing span, was 70 feet from its nose to its tail, and was 15 feet in height. It flew at a maximum speed of 250 miles per hour at an altitude of 10,000 feet.

The B-17 met or exceeded all of the Army Air Corps specifications for speed, climb, range, and load carrying. It did suffer a setback though in October of 1935 when a pilot neglected to unlock the elevators (a wing mechanism critical to creating lift of the aircraft) on takeoff and the prototype B-17 crashed at Dayton, Ohio's Wright Field. In spite of that incident, the Army Air Corps knew it had its heavy bomber of the future.

Over the next few years, the B-17 went through several modifications. The B-17B, which was flight tested in 1939,

flew from Seattle, Washington to New York City in nine hours and fourteen minutes. It was a new record for cross continental flight. Improvements and upgrades to the

The B-17, America's Flying Fortress.

engines, armament, and weaponry of the B-17 made it the most formidable aircraft in the sky. After the Japanese attacked the Pacific Fleet at Pearl Harbor, B-17C's and B-17D's were the first Flying Fortresses to see action in combat. Not long after its debut, B-17E's were produced in greater number with more formidable fifty-caliber waist and tail machine guns and powered turrets were added in the roof of the aircraft and under its fuselage. In the spring of 1942, an even faster plane with longer range and larger bomb load capacity rolled off the Boeing assembly line. General Henry "Hap" Arnold called the B-17, *the guts and backbone of our world-wide aerial offensive.*

Raymond was confident in his ability to lead his crew and successfully fly this formidable ship. He was more than just a pilot now. He had the title of Flight Commander. On the ground and in the air, he bore responsibility for the lives of as many as ten men under his command. They were trained professionals in their own fields of expertise as co-pilot, gunner, navigator, engineer, radio operator, and bombardier. When they were on that aircraft, the crew was like its own little army. Its commander needed to know each member of his crew as an individual, as well as understand their place as a component of that small army. Raymond's success as a commander was reliant upon his ability to secure the enduring trust of his crew, a difficult balance of earning the confidence of his men and demanding their respect, while instilling in each crewman the belief that he was still one of them.

Everything that Raymond learned through his train-ing was reapplied specifically to this aircraft. He studied its construction and all of its equipment. Flying this beast of an aircraft in formation, flying it at night, knowing how to crash land or ditch the B-17 and bail out of it if necessary,

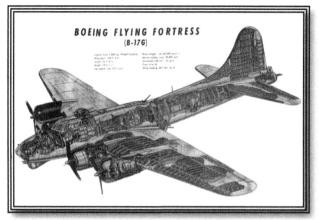

BOEING FLYING FORTRESS
(B-17G)

Cutaway profile of Boeing's B-17.

became second nature to him.

On many formation training flights, Raymond was selected to lead the formation and be at its point. On those days he told Helen to look up at the sky as the B-17's and support aircraft took to the heavens.

"Darling, watch the first plane when we take off today, the one at the head of the formation. That will be me."

He was so proud to lead and Helen was proud of him and all of the other guys up there. There were so many planes in the air some days; it looked as though the skies over Louisiana were completely filled with B-17s and other aircraft. During night training missions, there were more planes than stars.

Raymond and his crew were scheduled for transfer to the Grand Island Army Air Field in Nebraska on March 1, 1944. Grand Island was under the command of the Second Air Force. It was often the last stop for B-17 crews before receiving their final assignment for combat in the European Theater of World War II. Here, the crews received their final instructions and were equipped with the gear they would take with them overseas. It was the last place where they could have a couple of nights out on the town before seeing the enemy and combat for the first time.

A few nights of fun out with the boys in Nebraska was the last thing on Raymond's mind. Another heart wrenching goodbye was on the horizon. The evening before Raymond took off with his crew from Louisiana to Nebraska and ultimately on to their assignment overseas, he and Helen prepared for their last evening together. Helen, wearing a black apron over a white linen dress, her long dark hair up in a ponytail, was preparing a final home cooked meal of steak, potatoes, biscuits, and apple cobbler. Raymond quietly gathered and packed his belongings in their bedroom, readying for his departure early the next morning.

"Supper's ready, Raymond," Helen called as she placed their plates on the kitchen table.

When Raymond emerged from their bedroom, he paused momentarily. Helen noticed him gazing at her.

"What is it?" Helen asked him.

"I wrote a letter to my sister Marjorie when I first met you, darling. I told her that I had met the prettiest girl in New York City."

"Oh, that is so sweet, Raymond," Helen responded with a girlish grin on her face.

"But I was wrong, darling. I met the prettiest girl in the whole world that day."

"And you, my Raymond, are the most handsome and bravest soldier who ever put on a uniform." Helen gave Raymond a gentle kiss on the cheek.

They sat across from each other at the kitchen table and talked of their families and got caught up on the news from back home. Raymond had just received letters from his parents and sisters and Helen had recently gotten letters from two of her brothers and her mother. They shared their respective family stories and talked about the weather and most every other topic that came to mind, except for one... the war and

Raymond's destiny with it. There was time enough to worry about missions to be flown and battles to be fought after Raymond's departure the next morning.

After they finished eating supper, they washed and dried the dishes. As Raymond reached up to place the last of the plates, cups, and saucers in the kitchen cupboard, Helen slipped her arms around his waist and guided him out to the porch of their cabin. Helen sat in one of the two old, creaky wooden rockers on the porch and Raymond just stood there looking out in the direction of the airfield as B-17's took off in the twilight for night training flights. Helen watched her husband as he gazed up at the battleships of the sky lifting off the earth and heading toward the heavens. The airfield lights created a silhouette of Raymond who was more like a boy when she first met him in Central Park nearly two years earlier. Helen was just a girl herself, three months shy of her seventeenth birthday when they first set eyes on one another. Here he was now, broader in the shoulders and brimming with so much confidence and pride. Helen thought he might have even grown taller.

"Raymond, when did you first realize that you loved me?"

"The moment I looked into your eyes right after we ran into each other in Central Park."

"I knew that."

"Well, if you knew that, then why…?

"Because, I just wanted to hear you say it."

"And what about you, darling? When did you know we were meant for each other?"

Helen paused.

"When we met in the park I thought you were special."

"How special?"

"Very special, Raymond. But, when you kissed me on the front stoop after our first date, there was no doubt in my mind that we would spend the rest of our lives together."

Helen was happy and content. Raymond had slept by her side for the past five months and regardless of the frequent moves, tedious travel, and dilapidated accommodations they shared, these were the best five months of her life. And this was just the beginning. The advent of a lifetime together.

Raymond stepped away from the porch rail and pulled the other rocking chair next to Helen's. He sat and reached for her hand and their fingers instinctively intermingled. He told Helen that as excited as he was about joining the air corps, becoming a pilot, and doing his duty for his country, it was she who now filled his days with excitement and wonder.

Just as they had sat together until the wee hours of the morning on Helen's front stoop the night before Raymond left Helen in New York City in 1942 to continue his training, they sat together again, hoping against hope that they wouldn't really have to part.

There was little else said as their chairs rocked back and forth in unison and the floor boards of the old cabin porch creaked in concert with the chirps of the crickets. A faint whistling sound filled the air as a gentle breeze blew through the branches of a solitary southern magnolia tree. A yellow warbler serenaded them as the air grew chilly and their breath now came out as tiny clouds.

It was nearly two o'clock in the morning when Raymond glanced over at Helen, whose eyes appeared to be moistening with sadness. He stood up and lifted his petite love out of her chair and into his arms. He carried her inside to their bedroom, not knowing when next they would sleep by each other's side.

Even in paradise the sun sets. He put that thought to rest. For this night, they disregarded reality. They embraced each other, lost in the present and dreaming of their future together.

1880's • 1890's • 1900's • 1910's • 1920's • 1930's • 1940's • 1950's
↑
MARCH-JUNE 1944

Off to War

Oh little it is that we believe in
And much the faith we've lost;
Enough, perhaps, we share with MEN
The price that freedom costs.
— Anonymous

Pilot Raymond Stephenson was ordered to depart Grand Island, Nebraska on March 11, 1944. Joining him on a new B-17 were co-pilot Joe Ward, navigator Gene Swiatnicki, bombardier John Jameson, engineer Earl Westerholm, radio operator Joe Minery, and gunners Keith Clinton, Jacob Brinn and Irv Ogier. They flew to the Presque Isle Army Air Field in Maine and then on to Grenier Field in Manchester, New Hampshire, where they received their final instructions and orders for permanent assignment in Europe. On March 19th the crew of nine headed for combat.

The youngest was a mere eighteen years of age and the most senior member, Raymond, was just twenty-three. They took off from Grenier Field that day for a three-legged flight across the Atlantic Ocean, assigned to the 8th Air Force Service Command, European Theatre of Operations, in England. They flew the North Atlantic route with stops in Newfoundland, Canada and Reykjavik, Iceland for refueling. The crew also made a stop in Ireland. It was in Ireland that their brand new B-17 was confiscated and assigned to another crew that had an urgent mission. Now without an aircraft, Raymond and company traveled by train to the coast of Ireland and crossed the Irish Sea by ferry to England, arriving there on March 26, 1944.

This band of young airmen was assigned to the 652nd

Bombardment Squadron of the 25th Bombardment Group, 8th Air Force. The crew stayed for a short time in Boddington, England, where they conducted additional training flights and honed their gunnery skills before moving on to their permanent home at the Royal Air Force Station Watton in Norfolk, England. Watton was a sprawling facility with a two thousand yard long concrete runway that was used primarily as a bomber airfield by both the Royal Air Force and the United States Army Eighth Air Force.

At Watton the shiny new B-17 that the crew lost in Ireland was replaced. Raymond, Joe Ward, and Keith Clinton walked down to the airfield from their barracks to see their newly assigned aircraft.

"This old piece of junk can't be ours," Keith moaned.

"This is the worst looking pile of crap with wings and propellers I've ever seen," noted Joe. "What are we going to name her, Raymond?"

It was a common practice for a crew to name its aircraft, often after a woman in their lives, such as the Enola Gay, the Memphis Belle, or Manchester Misses. Raymond lifted his hand to his chin and pondered his answer to Joe's question for a minute.

"Gentlemen, I don't think any woman wants to be named after such an old, beat up pile of airborne scrap metal. Unless you have an ugly ex-girlfriend that you want to insult, I think we'll just let it be."

Brigadier General Elliott Roosevelt, son of President Franklin Delano Roosevelt, was the commanding officer of the 25th Bombardment Group. The operational objectives of the 25th Bombardment Group were generally of a reconnaissance nature. They flew more than 3,000 missions during the war. With the exception of chaff dispensing missions, a lone craft was assigned to carry out its mission. These solitary aircraft and crews flew weather, photography, and target scouting missions, as well as spy drops behind enemy lines. The group also flew electronic counter-measure missions, in which chaff, thin pieces of aluminum or metallized plastic that would appear as targets on enemy radar, was dispensed in the sky to confuse enemy radar defenses during Allied attacks.

For Raymond and the boys in his crew, the risks of flight were impossible to ignore. Nearly every day the number of dead and missing airmen grew. The fallen were not faceless names that appeared in a newspaper, or were recited during

Raymond and his crew, RAF Watton, 1944.
Front row from from right to left,
Pilot Raymond Stephenson, Co-pilot Joseph Ward,
Navigator Eugene Swiatnicki, one unidentified.
Back row from right to left, Engineer Earl Westerholm,
Gunner Leonard Licurse, Radio Operator Joseph Minery,
Gunner Keith Clinton, two unidentified.

a radio broadcast. The missing were the fellows that shared a barracks with them. The dead were their buddies with whom they chased down a cold beer while off duty. The airmen that were captured and confined to a Nazi hell hole of prisoner of war camp, were the same boys who played poker with them while waiting to hear word of where their next mission would take them.

They all knew that their next mission might be their last. Raymond had an added responsibility and greater burden as flight commander. One mistake, a single errant maneuver on his part, and not only would he jeopardize his own life, but those of the men he grew to respect as crewmates and love like brothers. Raymond never dwelled on death and was incurably optimistic. Others though, struggled to cope with the death they saw around them and the possibility that they might be next. Some of the guys were sure their number would eventually come up, while others considered themselves invincible. Some airmen coped through prayer and the power of positive thought, while others faced fear by lingering on the neck of a beer bottle, or a container of whatever brand of hooch they could acquire on base.

The 652nd Bombardment Squadron missions were perilous. A successful mission required skill, imagination, endurance, and courage. Many missions penetrated enemy occupied territory. Some involved flying for up to fifteen consecutive hours at altitudes as low as fifty feet above the surface of the Atlantic Ocean and as high as thirty-five thousand feet. Icing and bone chillingly cold temperatures posed risks to both the aircraft and the crew at such heights. At their lowest elevations, underestimating the height of the ocean's waves and swells could swamp an aircraft. Given the frigid temperatures of the North Atlantic Ocean, the likelihood of surviving long enough if you wound up in the drink until help arrived was extremely remote.

When Raymond and his crew took to the skies, they were alone. No other bomber or fighter escorts accompanied them. To allow the crew to go on extended missions, the explosive arsenal that commonly occupied the bomb bays, was replaced with additional fuel tanks. A crash, hard landing, or an enemy round striking the bomb bay fuel tanks could turn a B-17 into an instant inferno, giving the crew little or no chance of escape or survival. The size of the normal B-17 crew was reduced by at least two members. One gunner was eliminated along with the bombardier, for whom they had no use.

Despite the lighter crew, the total weight of the aircraft for these missions was substantially heavier. The plane carried the full complement of guns and ammunition and although the arsenal of bombs was not present on the aircraft, at roughly six pounds per gallon, the extra fuel load added so much weight that it pushed the overall burden of the B-17 to the very upper limit of what its straining engines could lift into the air. On take-off, if an engine faltered, the consequences could be disastrous.

Missions were flown around the clock and were critical to the efforts and success of the 8th Air Force and the Allied Forces. Reconnaissance aircraft and crews from the Mighty Eighth were instrumental in the planning and execution of the D-Day invasion at Normandy, France on June 6, 1944.

Hazards were plentiful. In addition to the explosion and fire hazards of the maximum fuel loads carried on their B-17, the effects of fatigue on long flights increased the likelihood of pilot or crew error. As an aircraft glided above the North

Atlantic at night at altitudes below fifty feet, the pilot could not see the waves and swells of the ocean. They flew so low over the sea that the crew members in the waist of the plane could taste the saltiness of the spray of the ocean water. There was virtually no margin for error. Reconnaissance mission crews flew routes and employed strategies to avoid trouble. But in war, trouble has a way of finding you.

On a cold and overcast April night over the North Atlantic Ocean just off the European coast, Raymond and his crew were cruising at an altitude of thirty thousand feet. Their mission orders directed them to obtain certain atmospheric and meteorological readings in preparation for a bombing mission over Europe. The aircraft had to navigate the extremes of altitude range, dropping from their thirty thousand foot perch, down to near sea level.

The clouds were so thick; visibility was limited to a few feet. As they let down through the clouds, it wasn't until they dropped below a thousand feet, that the clouds and fog thinned and visibility began to improve. No one on board liked what they saw. Just below them was an enemy ship convoy. No sooner had they spotted the convoy of German warships, the sky was bursting with flares. Flak was coming at them. Exploding metal filled the sky. All aboard were jolted by the barrage of flak launched from the Nazi ships below, erupting all around their B-17. The only protections they had were the skills of their gunners and the cunning of their pilot.

"Ray, get us the hell outta' here," Joe Minery shouted into his radio.

Their pilot was already on it. Raymond pitched the B-17's nose upward, gaining altitude as fast as possible at full throttle. The engines screamed and strained as the aircraft climbed.

The g-force gripped the crew as they abruptly ascended. The sky grew quieter as they reached higher elevations. That wasn't necessarily a good sign. Enemy ships routinely halted their flak attacks to clear the sky for their own aircraft to strike back. Raymond stayed in the clouds and sped away as fast as the B-17's engines would propel it. The aircraft was plunked a few times by flak, but escaped with little damage and no crew injuries.

The crew realized that each time they flew a mission they might get shot down. If their ship was crippled over the ocean and they had to bail out, they might drown in the drink, become shark bait, or be recovered by the enemy and rot in a POW camp… or worse. Incidents like this couldn't get into their heads. They shook them off as best they could to prepare mentally for the next mission. Co-pilot Joe Ward would get on the intercom and wisecrack after an attack.

"I'm starting to think that someone doesn't like us."

Off duty, the guys would try to relax. Keith Clinton bought an old, used bicycle he enjoyed riding around the Watton air base. Some of the other fellows liked to play cards and write letters home. Joe Minery was friendly with some of his British counterparts and they invited him on a fox hunt, about which he was very excited. However, after a full day on the hunt, Joe returned to his quarters whining and grumbling.

"What's eating you?" Keith Clinton asked as Joe moped around the barracks.

"The Britishers said I can't fox hunt with them anymore."

"Why not?"

"They said I was ungentlemanly. I guess when you spot the fox you're supposed to call out, *Tally-ho*, not *C'mon, let's get that son of a bitch*."

On May 9, 1944, the crew was assigned to their next mission. They were up and out of their bunks early, had breakfast and were briefed on the mission and its objectives. They boarded their B-17 with a limited crew. Raymond was at the controls with Joe Ward, as usual, in the co-pilot's seat. Gene Swiatnicki was on board as navigator, engineer Earl Westerholm was seated in the belly of the craft, and Joe Minery parked himself at the radio man's position. Keith Clinton occupied his usual role as one of the gunners and Eddie Walden pinch hit in the other gunner's position, replacing a sick crew member. Dave Mulligan, a member of the British meteorology team, joined them.

Raymond taxied onto the runway and was given final clearance to take off. He fired up the engines and gave it the gun. The engines roared, the ship shook and barreled down the runway before lifting off and heading skyward. The mission was a long one that took the crew out to the Azores, an archipelago of nine volcanic islands west of Portugal in the Atlantic Ocean. British naval and air bases were located there under a lease from Portugal to the British Empire. It was a key facility for the Allied Forces. It gave them a base from which air support could protect convoys and detect the movements of enemy naval vessels and aircraft.

The mission was routine on the first leg heading away from England. The mission's goal was to take meteorological readings and gather reconnaissance information over the Atlantic. The average length of these missions exceeded twelve hours of flight time and flying at elevations ranging from fifty feet to thirty thousand feet. The work of this unit and others like it, determined whether or not hundreds or thousands of other Allied aircraft would launch to attack enemy targets across Europe. Their reconnaissance results and recommendations determined the day and time that the ships of the navy, combat aircraft of the air forces, and ground troops of the army and Marines would attack critical targets. These missions were critical to the success of the invasion of Europe and the eventual Allied victory.

On their return trip from the Azores, the crew was approximately two hundred miles from Land's End. While always aware and vigilant, they were also relaxed. Keith Clinton was a tall man and he hoisted himself out of the tail gunner's post to stretch his long legs. Eddie Walden came up out of the ball gun turret and joined him in the waist of the Flying Fortress to grab a cup of coffee. Eddie and Keith sat, sipped their coffee and looked forward to a smooth, uneventful flight back to Watton and a hot meal upon their return.

Bam, bam, bam! Three rapid, successive explosions rocked the aircraft. The horrible sound of metal shredding and the rattling of the ship rousted them up. Bullets and twenty-millimeter shells ripped through the fuselage and the windows of the plane. Peering out the windows, the crew saw they were under attack by four German JU-88 aircraft that had come up from behind and underneath their B-17. The twin engine multi-role JU-88 was one of the most versatile weapons of the German Luftwaffe and a key asset in its deadly arsenal.

Keith Clinton was struck and wounded in the back of the head. It could have been worse for him, though. The first rounds fired by the Nazi JU-88's that struck the B-17 were direct hits on the tail gun position. If Keith hadn't come up to the waist of the plane to stretch out and have a cup of coffee, he would have been killed. Eddie was wounded next, taking a hit in the back.

Raymond took defensive maneuver measures. Radio operator Joe Minery sent May Day calls out. As Joe desperately called for help, he noticed blood oozing from Keith's head and the crimson drops trickling down his neck. Keith appeared to be dazed, but suddenly snapped out of it. He raised his head up and glanced over at the radio station.

"Patch me up, Joe!"

Joe wrapped up Keith's head in rolls of bandages as best he could. The bleeding wouldn't stop, but at least it slowed. Keith, a skilled gunner, was determined to engage the enemy in spite of his wound.

"Help me get down into the ball turret, Joe."

Meteorologist Dave Mulligan, although not extensively trained as a gunner, grabbed one of the waist guns and started delivering a barrage of fifty-caliber machine gun shells on the enemy. Mad as hell, Eddie Walden fought off the pain from the wound he suffered to his back and manned another gun.

"Some Nazi son of a bitch is gonna' pay for this!"

The air battle lasted almost thirty minutes. In spite of the four aircraft to one advantage of the Nazi attackers, the firepower of the Flying Fortress and the extraordinary tactics employed by its pilot and gunners, dissuaded their Nazi assailants from continuing their aerial assault. One Nazi JU-88 was critically damaged and plunged into the cold, dark waters of the Atlantic. Another JU-88 flew off leaving a trail of smoke from damage inflicted by the Fortress' sharp shooting gunners.

Despite the respite from the attack, the crew still wasn't out of trouble. Unbeknownst to the rest of the crew at the time, Raymond was wounded during the attack, taking a shot or shrapnel in his left thigh. With nearly one hundred miles to go until reaching Land's End, there was severe damage to the tail of the plane. A shell had blown a hole clear through it, making the craft unstable. British Spitfires, responding to Joe Minery's May-Day calls, arrived to escort them back to England.

The pilot of one of the escorting British Spitfires radioed the nearly crippled B-17 with some more bad news. Both sets of the B-17's landing gear were destroyed. The crew, peering out the windows, found more trouble. Minery radioed his pilot.

"Raymond, we got two engines out and a third smoking."

"I know, Joe."

"How the hell are we gonna' get back?"

"If you know any prayers Joe, start saying them."

As the aircraft rumbled closer toward Land's End, it began to lose altitude rapidly. They couldn't make it to an airfield. Raymond concluded that the only option he had to save his crew, was to put his B-17 down on its belly on as soft and as smooth a surface as he could find near Land's End.

He took visual inventory of the land below, looking for surfaces with large, delineated squares that typically were flat farm fields. He was woozy from the fatigue of the long flight, the air battle, and loss of blood from his wound. He caught sight of a spot that might be long enough and flat enough to put his airship down on its belly. Seconds later, he realized he was not going to make it that far. Any spot without buildings or thick forestation would have to do. The B-17 was dropping fast.

The crew readied for a crash landing. Joe Minery noticed that Keith Clinton was unconscious in the ball gun turret in the belly of the plane. That's the last place a crew member wanted to be when the bottom of the aircraft collides with the earth. Joe Ward leaped out of the co-pilot's seat and he and Minery dragged Clinton out of the ball gun turret. They laid him on the floor in the waist of the plane and strapped him down. The rest of the crew buckled up for a rough landing.

Stephenson gave three commands as he prepared to land.

"Hunker down, buckle up, and say a prayer."

The crew took some comfort in knowing that Raymond was at the controls. Not to say that the other pilots weren't top notch aviators, for many were. However, they knew ice water ran through his veins. He never got rattled. No one ever saw him lose his cool. If anyone could land this old bucket of flying junk with only half a tail, half its engines out, no landing gear, and a fuselage that looked like Swiss cheese, it was Raymond.

He spotted an area that appeared to be as flat and as soft a surface as he was going to find and that his aircraft might possibly reach. He continued to lose altitude rapidly as he approached his target. He fought to keep the nose of the aircraft up and keep it straight. BOOM… THWACK! Abruptly, the bottom of the fuselage hit the Land's End sod. It jolted everyone on board. The aircraft bounced off the earth's surface and was momentarily airborne again. Grass, dirt and every manner of foliage was strewn all over and around the aircraft. Raymond managed to keep the craft in a fairly straight line with little help from its badly damaged tail and obliterated landing gear. If he could avoid a spin or manage not to flip the plane, they had a chance. The plane scraped and scoured the ground for several hundred feet and eventually came to a halt. A quick evacuation was critical. A possible explosion from a fuel leak and fire threatened all of the crew.

The wounded and unconscious Keith Clinton, blood still dripping from his head, was carried from the plane by his crew mates. So too was Eddie Walden, who writhed in pain from his back wound and was incapable of walking. British meteorologist Dave Mulligan was also wounded. He was struck near his throat with a bursting twenty-millimeter shell or a piece of shrapnel that tore into his flesh, creating a severe laceration that bled profusely. Despite being hobbled by the wound to his leg, Raymond, along with Joe Ward, Joe Minery, and Gene Swiatnicki, helped carry the wounded. They laid their injured crewmates on the ground a safe distance from the badly damaged and smoking aircraft. Ambulances and medical help arrived on the scene. Clinton, Mulligan, Walden and Raymond, were transported by the "meat wagon" to the Land's End Royal Air Force Base dispensary for treatment. As the medical vehicles drove off, Joe Ward looked over at his flight engineer.

"Earl. For Christ's sake, you're bleeding."

Earl was struck by shrapnel. During the mayhem of the aerial assault and subsequent crash landing, he hadn't noticed he was wounded.

In reports given in the aftermath of the attack and crash landing, Raymond was praised for his outstanding evasive maneuvering skills while engaged in the sky high battle with the four German JU-88's. He was also commended for successfully landing the badly damaged B-17 without causing any additional injuries or any fatalities to his crew.

The old B-17 to which they were assigned had been described by some of the crew as an *old piece of junk* and a *bucket of rusted bolts*. But, it somehow managed to fly despite being shredded with gunfire, losing two of its four engines and a good bit of its tail. Sure, the flying skills of its flight commander had a lot to do with delivering the crew back to Land's End alive, but in spite of its age and condition, this particular Flying Fortress held together. The crew had a new-found respect for their aircraft. Maybe she deserved a name after all. Lucky Lady perhaps?

During World War II nearly 13,000 B-17's were built. Almost 5,000 of them were lost during the war. The B-17 was so critical a weapon and made such a significant contribution toward the Allied victory, that General Carl A. Spaatz, who commanded the United States Army Air Forces in Great Britain, gave it great praise.

"Without the B-17, we might have lost the war."

A repair crew was sent down from the Watton Royal Air Force base to the site of the emergency landing to repair the B-17 and put it back in service. Repair and salvage crews concluded that the aircraft *looked like a sieve* and was *unsalvageable*. They and the crew looking at that B-17 after the crash, thought it was a miracle that anyone could land it safely in that condition. Raymond, though, gave credit to being blessed with a great plane and brave crew, who despite their wounds and long odds, fought off four attacking enemy aircraft. He also gave thanks to God for looking over them as he clutched a small pocket Bible his mother had given him. He always carried it in the pocket of his flight uniform. A similar Bible was the constant occupant of a uniform pocket of Gunner Keith Clinton. They were chided at times for never being parted from their Bibles. Raymond's response to the ribbing was to recite a verse from the Book of Daniel:

> *...the people who know their God will carry out great exploits!*

Within a few days, the entire crew was back at the Watton Royal Air Force base, except for Keith Clinton and Eddie

Walden, whose wounds required them to stay and convalesce in an Army field hospital near Land's End for about two weeks. They were told that at the end of their two week hospital stay, they would be re-assigned to light duty at the hospital. Keith and Eddie knew that light duty was a euphemism for peeling potatoes and ladling soup, also known as KP (kitchen police) duty. They were anxious to return to Watton with the rest of the crew and get back in the air. They charmed one of the nurses into sending a telegram to their commanding officer, Lieutenant Colonel Joseph Stenglein, telling him that they were fit for duty. Two days later into the infirmary walked Lieutenant Colonel Stenglein, two captains, and four enlisted men. Against the advice and objections of the field hospital staff, they brought Keith and Eddie back to the hospital in Watton.

Eddie and Keith were discharged after a two-day stay at the Watton Hospital and were cleared for return to duty. Feeling fully recovered, Keith wanted to ride his bike around the base. As he looked in the vicinity of his barracks for his bicycle, he spotted a British soldier riding off with it.

"Hey buddy. Where do you think you're going with my bike?" Keith called out to him.

"Your bicycle? This is my bicycle."

"The hell it is! That's my bike," Keith responded.

"The hell it is. A couple of blokes in your barracks told me last week that the chap who owned this bike was killed in the crash of their B-17 near Land's End. They sold it to me."

For the wounds in battle which they had suffered, Raymond Stephenson, Keith Clinton, Earl Westerholm, Eddie Walden, and Dave Mulligan all were awarded the Purple Heart. In addition, on June 5, 1944, famed World War II air commander, General James (Jimmy) H. Doolittle issued the following order:

> *For extraordinary achievement, while piloting a B-17 airplane on a weather reconnaissance mission over enemy patrolled waters on 9 May 1944. Four enemy fighters made a sudden attack on his craft, knocking out two engines, setting one ablaze. Maneuvering the stricken plane with exceptional skill, Lieutenant Stephenson employed violent evasive tactics, enabling his gunners to bring their fire to bear on the attackers. During this savage battle, five members of the crew were wounded, the entire tail assembly and control cables severely damaged, the hydraulic system rendered useless and both tires punctured. Exhibiting courage, sound judgment and superior airmanship, Lieutenant Stephenson fought his way back to England and despite the damaged condition of his aircraft accomplished a safe landing.*

By order of General Doolittle, the Distinguished Flying Cross was awarded to First Lieutenant Clarence R. Stephenson for his gallantry, courage and superior airmanship in keeping with the highest traditions of the Army Air Forces.

1880's • 1890's • 1900's • 1910's • 1920's • 1930's • 1940's • 1950's

MARCH-AUGUST 1944

She Never Saw It Coming

Life is a flame that is always burning itself out,
but it catches fire again every time a child is born.
— George Bernard Shaw

Helen missed all the signs. Then again, no one ever told her what the signs were. Some mornings she was nauseous and vomited. She chalked that up to the quality of food she ate while at military facilities and when she was traveling. It could have been motion sickness caused by her train rides, or maybe the fumes she inhaled while riding on old buses across the country that made her sick. She was putting on a bit of weight, even though she had trouble keeping her breakfast down. That must have come from not being as active as she was while growing up, running around the streets of New York City and playing in Central Park she rationalized. Her menstrual cycle was interrupted. She didn't care what the reason was for that. Anything that could stop "the curse" from coming every month was a welcome relief.

Now back on 47th Street after Raymond's departure for Europe, Helen mentioned her symptoms to her mother.

"Helen, you are blessed with child," Maggie informed her. Helen was all at once thrilled, yet frightened.

"I'm going to have a baby? Oh Mom. What do I do? How do I…?"

"Hush, Helen. This is a good and blessed circumstance. A gift from God for you and Raymond. It will be fine."

Maggie brought Helen to one of the few women doctors in their neighborhood to confirm what she believed to be Helen's condition and to have the doctor explain everything about being with child that Helen needed to know. Having given birth to four children herself, Maggie was no stranger to this topic, but she was uneasy discussing such a delicate issue with her daughter, just as she had been about discussing wedding night matters.

Helen regretted not being able to tell Raymond in person that he was going to be a father. The day her pregnancy was confirmed, she sat at the kitchen table and wrote a letter to her husband.

> *Dear Raymond,*
>
> *I have the most wonderful news. I am going to be a mother and you are going to be a father! I am doing just fine. Mom took me to see a lady doctor and she says that the baby should be born sometime this summer (1944). If it is a boy, I would like to call him Raymond. I thought you would like that name. I like the name Ann Marie if it is a girl. The next time you write to me, let me know if you like those names too.*
>
> *I miss you very much my Raymond and hope you are safe. I pray for you every night before I go to sleep and you are the first thing I think of every morning when I wake up. I know you are very busy, but please write to me whenever you get a chance. I love to receive your letters.*

Please keep yourself safe. You will soon have two people to come home to who miss you and need you. God be with you.

I Love You - Helen

Helen's pregnancy was uneventful, until of course the time came when she went into labor. Helen's brother Marty, who at the time was in the Army Signal Corp, was temporarily assigned to the Army News Service and working in New York City. When Helen went into labor, Marty took her to Saint Clare's Hospital, four blocks away on 51st Street where the baby would be delivered. He promised to stay with her until the baby was born. While the delivery process had been explained to Helen, she had little idea how painful it could be or how long it might take.

Helen agonized through twenty hours of labor. It was late July and the delivery room was stifling hot. Sweat poured from her head. Every pore of her body perspired, soaking her hospital gown. Helen wasn't sure how much she could take, as her contractions and the pain associated with them left her breathless and exhausted. One of the attendants in the maternity ward was a nun. Helen cried in pain.

"Oh dear God, please help me."

"Stop carrying on like that and taking the Lord's name in vain," the nun scolded. "Don't make me call Mother Alice to come in here to speak to you!"

Helen flashed back to when she was a girl and sent to the principal's office at St. Michael's School to be chastised for inappropriate behavior and threatened with the cat o' nine tails. She struggled to muffle her cries.

As she continued to battle through the delivery process, Helen heard a doctor tell a nurse that if the baby was not delivered soon, they would have to take the baby. Helen asked her brother Marty, who was peeking in on her from time to time, what taking the baby meant.

"That means they will open your stomach and pull the baby out."

"Oh no. No one's opening me up."

Helen was determined to deliver her child. She used every bit of strength to push and as she entered her twenty first hour of labor, a final exhausting and painful push, produced a beautiful, healthy, baby girl.

After cleaning the baby, a nurse placed her in Helen's arms. She cradled and rocked her daughter in her arms, listening to the sound of her first cries. Helen counted to ten as she inventoried all of her fingers and toes. She was perfect.

Marty was watching through an open door as Helen delivered. He may have succumbed to exhaustion, the heat, or the sight of a baby passing from his little sister, but he passed out and hit the floor like a sack of potatoes. The thud of Marty hitting the floor alerted a nurse. She waved smelling salts under his nostrils for a few seconds and Marty awakened. He was helped up off the delivery room floor and escorted to a chair. In the meantime, because the Gregg's did not have a telephone, an orderly from the hospital walked over to 47th Street to tell Maggie that she had a new granddaughter. The orderly told her she should come by the hospital to see her daughter and granddaughter, as well as to escort her son home.

As she had told Raymond in the letter she sent when her pregnancy was confirmed, she named their angelic new daughter Ann Marie. Helen, although physically and mentally drained from the ordeal of delivery, was euphorically re-energized. She was overcome with affection for Ann Marie and the extraordinary love she felt for Raymond was deepened. Although he was thousands of miles away, a part of him was cradled in Helen's arms. It was just a day later after arriving home from the hospital, that Helen wrote to Raymond again to tell him that he was now the father of a precious baby girl.

When Ann Marie was about four weeks old, in late August 1944, Helen wanted to send a photograph of her and Ann Marie to the Watton Royal Air Force Base so Raymond could see a picture of his lovely baby girl. Cameras, like irons, rubber gloves, tools and many other common items and commodities, were hard to come by during the war. They were rationed as was food. All part of the war effort. Helen had difficulty finding a new camera, especially one that she could afford. Out of desperation, she went to a pawn shop on 10ᵗʰ Avenue located around the corner from her apartment building. Luckily, she was able to buy a used camera there. The pawn shop owner threw in a roll of film for free. Helen asked her youngest brother, Johnny, to accompany her to the roof of their tenement building to take a picture of her and Ann Marie.

Helen put on her nicest dress. She dressed Ann Marie in the baby gown and hat in which she was baptized. After Johnny took the photograph, Helen brought the film to have it developed. With the photograph in hand, she returned to the apartment and sat down at the kitchen table with Johnny to compose a letter for Raymond to accompany the photograph. It could be several days if not weeks before Raymond might receive the picture and letter and write back to her.

"Johnny, you took a beautiful picture."

"You and Ann Marie look great in it."

"I hope this letter and picture get to Raymond by September sixth. It's our first wedding anniversary."

"It's your birthday too, right?"

"Yes. This picture of me and Ann Marie would be the perfect anniversary gift for my Raymond."

Helen with her daughter Ann Marie
on the roof of their 47th Street tenement, 1944.

1880's • 1890's • 1900's • 1910's • 1920's • 1930's • 1940's • 1950's

↑

SEPTEMBER 1944

Mission: Code Name Epicure

Let me not mourn for the men who have died fighting,
but rather let me be glad that such heroes have lived.
— General George S. Patton

O n the afternoon of September 6, 1944, 1st Lieutenant and Flight Commander Raymond Stephenson and his crew received a briefing for a mission that would take them along the European Atlantic coast and out to the Azores archipelago that night. Joining Raymond on this mission was the usual gang, his co-pilot, Joe Ward; navigator, Eugene Swiatnicki; engineer, Earl Westerholm; radio operator Joe Minery; meteorologist Marv Rogers, and gunners Lenny Licurse and Keith Clinton.

After the briefing, the crew sat together to eat supper before heading out on their mission. As much as Raymond loved flying and serving his country, there was no other place he wanted to be on this particular day, his first wedding anniversary and his beloved wife's birthday, than back home with Helen and his six-week-old baby girl, Ann Marie.

This mission, code named Epicure, would be a long affair. The assignment would exceed fifteen hours of flight time. As was the case many times before, this was an unescorted reconnaissance mission under the cover of darkness. In order to cover the considerable distance required to complete this operation, the payload and bomb ordinance that customarily occupied the bomb bays, was replaced with additional fuel tanks. The crew was scheduled for departure at 2245 hours. It was a clear, cool evening with visibility up to six miles and winds out of the southeast at four miles per hour. Ideal flying conditions.

Once the crew had their fill at supper, they walked together down to the flight line toward their airplane. The ground and flight crews gave the B-17 a thorough check inside and out. The crew boarded the aircraft and took their usual positions for takeoff, except for Lenny Licurse, who opted to sit up front near the flight deck, instead of back toward the radio room with his fellow gunner. Raymond was at the controls.

Right on schedule after methodically completing the entire pre-flight checklist, Raymond taxied around the perimeter of the runway. The aircraft came to a full stop at the end of the airstrip awaiting clearance for takeoff. Raymond loved to get behind the controls of his B-17. As exciting as he thought it would be when he dreamed of being a pilot as a high school boy, sitting in the cockpit and lifting this extraordinary aircraft into the sky was an experience that exceeded all of his youthful expectations.

Now in proper position and given clearance to take off, Raymond and his crew were ready to roll. Joe Minery was on the interphone and heard the click of the command set. He immediately turned to command channel and heard Stephenson call the tower.

"Ready for take-off."

Minery turned to gunner Keith Clinton and meteorologist Marv Rogers.

"We're off again, fellas. Just three more missions and we get to go home."

Minery was sitting on the small seat in front of the radio man's table. Clinton was seated on top of an A-3 bag (aviator's kit/duffel bag) and Rogers was seated on the aluminum food kit box. They were the only three crew members aft in the aircraft.

The engines were run up again and Stephenson gave it the gun. After an initial lurch, the Flying Fortress gathered momentum and accelerated down the runway. The ride along the airstrip was bumpy, but typical for a B-17 take-off. The sound of the engines was good and the speed of the aircraft more than adequate as it barreled down the runway. The shaking and rattling of a rolling behemoth of an airplane on the concrete air strip smoothed and dissipated as the Flying Fortress lifted off the ground and headed skyward.

Moments later, Marv Rogers heard an explosion above the roar of the engines. He felt a forceful, jarring sensation. In the darkness, peering through the radio man's compartment window, he saw bursts of light and flames. A powerful jolt knocked Keith Clinton off the A-3 bag. As he lay on his back on the floor of the aircraft, he saw flashes of fire outside through the windows of the B-17. Joe Minery was shaken by the severe trauma to their aircraft too.

"What the hell is going on?" Joe screamed into the radio.

The plane began to shake even more violently.

George McNerney, a British army private who was assigned to the Watton Royal Air Force Base ground security squad, was performing a routine security check and inspection of the Ack Ack site, a battery of anti-aircraft guns located beyond the end of the runway from which Raymond and his crew lifted off. As he was in the process of inspecting the hut and gun emplacements, McNerny heard a loud sputtering of an engine or engines, followed by a louder roar. When he looked in the direction from which he heard the violent eruption, he saw a B-17 flying erratically at low altitude. There appeared to be fire, or terrific exhaust flame from the motors on the left side of the plane.

Inside the thirty-two ton Flying Fortress, the crew heard a command shouted from Joe Ward in the flight deck.

"Brace yourselves!"

There was a sudden loss of altitude and everyone was tossed about the aircraft. The crewmen felt their stomachs come up through their throats as the plane plummeted. Keith Clinton tried to gird himself against a fuselage support column, but couldn't. He was thrown through a door to the waist of the plane and landed face first on the ball gun turret. He grabbed ahold of the ball turret and could feel the vibrations of the underbelly of the aircraft, first slamming against the earth and then dragging along the terrain. As Marvin Rogers saw Clinton fall through the door into the waist of the plane, he was knocked to the deck by the collision of the aircraft with the ground. As their B-17 skidded and grinded along the earth, Marv saw flames shoot up through the bomb bay doors, even though the bomb bay doors were closed.

"Holy shit. It's like a goddamn blow torch."

Joe Minery gripped the brace of the radio room escape hatch as the plane violently met the earth below. The strength of his grasp was no match for the force of the collision. His body was slammed against the radio room desk and chair.

Private McNerny, still standing at the Ack Ack site, saw the aircraft plunge. One wing of the plane struck a large oak tree as it plummeted toward the ground. The aircraft struck the earth with a thunderous sound. The ground shook as all sixty-five thousand pounds of the bomber's girth bounced and skidded across the English turf. Parts of the ship began to tear up, as a wing hit an anti-aircraft turret and the friction of the aircraft scraping against the ground sent the sounds of bending, tearing and shearing metal into the night. The B-17 finally ground to a halt, with the engines of the left wing fully enveloped in flames.

The fields and woods surrounding the fallen aircraft were littered with the guts of the B-17. Thousands of gallons of fuel and hydraulic fluid were oozing out of the plane, spreading over the area and seeping into the earth. The same highly flammable and volatile fluids escaping their fractured containers leaked throughout the interior of the aircraft, intermingling with the blood of injured crewmen. Bits and pieces of the wings, engines and fuselage were strewn about, transforming a once pristine meadow into a burning collection of debris.

Keith Clinton was lying on the floor of the waist of the aircraft as it grinded to a complete stop. Although dazed and battered, he picked himself up off the floor. Seeing that the plane was on fire, he forced open the waist outside door, seeking to escape the flames.

"Joe, Marv, this way. Let's get the hell outta' here!" Clinton yelled as he dove through the waist door to escape the spreading inferno.

"Keith, your hair's on fire!" Minery called out, just a step behind Clinton.

Marv Rogers, bruised, bloodied, and disoriented, wobbled through the smoke and darkness trying to follow his crewmate's voices. He stumbled to the waist door and crawled out on his hands and knees. The three crewmates clung close to the ground and looked back at the aircraft for Raymond, Joe, Earl, Gene, and Lenny. There was no sign of them outside the plane.

Their hearts and their guts told them they had to try to re-enter the aircraft to get to the flight deck and pilot compartment, but their B-17 was completely enveloped in flames from the bomb bay doors all the way to the nose of the aircraft.

Singed and pummeled from the crash, Clinton, Minery and Rogers were still not out of danger. In addition to the risk of an explosion that might occur on the plane, thousands of fifty-caliber ammunition rounds for the B-17's machine guns were still on board and commenced firing as the heat and flames reached them. Exploding ammunition intended for the enemy, was now coming their way. The three dropped into a nearby ditch and watched helplessly as the engines burned and the surplus tanks in the bomb bays erupted in flames. Their five friends and brothers-in-arms were still unaccounted for. Keith Clinton peeked up over the edge of their earthen shelter. He could see the flight deck through the smoke and flames.

"Oh my God."

"What is it, Keith?" Marv asked.

"Raymond and Joe. They're slumped over the controls in the cockpit."

Minery poked his head up.

"We gotta do something."

"It's too late Joe." Marv wept. "Dammit all. It's just too late. Only one thing left to do."

Keith, Minery and Marv crouched in that dirt hole and prayed for Raymond, Joe, Gene, Earl and Lenny.

Private McNerney, who had just witnessed the sequence of tragic events unfold, ran from his post toward the burning hulk of metal after it came to a rest. Seeing that the seventy-five-foot-long aircraft was in flames from the waist forward, he ran toward the tail of the ship. There was a huge hole in the rear of the fuselage into which he crawled.

"Is anybody in here?" McNerney shouted.

He went in a little further toward the waist, just a few steps and then heard gas explosions. He jumped back quickly, stuck his head out of the left side of the ship and saw flames all over the outside of the forward section. He heard a single blood curdling scream that died out immediately. The heat became so intense that he hurriedly left the aircraft the same way he went in, through the large opening in the rear. As he ran, he looked back to see if there were any bodies around. He found three men lying in a ditch about thirty yards from the ship. They were disoriented and disheveled.

Officers, enlisted men, and civilians began to arrive at the crash site in droves along with medical officers, ambulances and fire fighters. Ammunition and flares on board the aircraft continued to detonate. Keith, Marv and Minery were able to crawl from their ditch toward awaiting medical staff. They were taken by ambulance to the base hospital. Miraculously, they suffered only minor injuries.

The flames emanating from the wreckage of the aircraft were not extinguished completely until 2:30 a.m. the following morning on September 7th. Private McNerney, along with a detail of other soldiers, remained on guard of the smoldering remains of the airplane throughout the night. They searched the immediate area of the crash once the flames were completely extinguished in hope of finding additional crew members that may have escaped the crash and the subsequent inferno. Sadly, their efforts were in vain.

At about 10:00 a.m. the morning of September 7, Private McNerney, accompanied by the officer of the day, Captain

Nimmo and a handful of medical enlisted men, entered the fallen B-17. They removed the bodies of Raymond, Joe, Earl, Gene and Lenny, from what was left of their aircraft. Raymond's military medical records revealed that he suffered a compound fracture of one arm as a result of the crash. The cause of death was from the smoke and fire.

The five dead crew members were buried in the United States Military Cemetery in Cambridge, England. Keith, Marv, and Minery attended the graveside funeral service. They prayed for their friends. They cried as the flags draped over their caskets were folded, the bugler played taps and their crewmates were lowered into the earth. Soldiers talk about being brothers-in-arms. These crewmen **were** like brothers. They'd sacrifice their lives for each other.

After the funeral, all three of them returned to the crash site.

"I still don't believe it," Minery said as he overlooked the scene of the crash, flanked by Marv and Keith.

"I can't figure out what the hell happened," Marv said.

"Does it really matter?" Keith asked as he fought off another round of tears. "Could have been shot at. Might have been sabotage. Maybe it was just an accident. Thing is, no matter what took us down, Joe, Earl, Lenny, Raymond, and Gene are gone."

Keith raised his chin until his face was cast skyward. His eyes stared into the heavens.

"I love those guys."

1880's • 1890's • 1900's • 1910's • 1920's • 1930's • 1940's • 1950's

↑

Sᴇᴘᴛᴇᴍʙᴇʀ 1944

The Telegram

No farewell words were spoken,
No time to say goodbye.
You were gone before we knew it,
And only God knows why.

— *Anonymous*

R uth Stephenson, Raymond's youngest sister, was a sixteen-year-old girl and in her junior year at Ironton High School. At the end of the school day one late September afternoon, she walked home with some friends to her family's house on Seventh Street. As she approached the modest craftsman style abode that her father had built, it looked like her father's car was parked on the street nearby. It struck her as unusual, because she always got home from school well before her dad ever got home from work. He always worked well into the afternoon or early evening. Maybe that car belonged to someone else and just looks the same as her father's car. Ruth entered the house.

"Hi, I'm home."

There was no response. The red oak floors creaked as she walked through the living room, past the floral print sofa, toward the kitchen, where on most days after school, she expected to see her mother. On this day, however, she found her father sitting at the kitchen table. She wondered if he was sick or something was wrong. Her father was never home that early.

"Hi Dad. What are you doing home so early?"

Her father looked up from the kitchen table and turned toward his youngest child. Ruth could see that the whites of her dad's eyes were red, the perimeters swollen. His skin had an ashen tone. He never looked so distraught. His expression bordered on hopelessness. Not even during the great flood that nearly consumed their home, or during the times when they had no money and little to eat, did her father ever look so disheartened.

"Dad, what's wrong?"

Clarence Stephenson was a man who always exhibited a quiet strength and confident leadership in his family and his community. He was a rock and a steadying influence whether among the boy scouts he mentored, the Sunday school students he taught, his fellow soldiers during the First World War, or among his wife and three children. At this moment though, he had no answers. No words to share with Ruth.

He lifted a trembling hand from the surface of the kitchen table and pointed to a small sheet of paper on the laminate kitchen counter near the white ceramic sink. Ruth walked slowly over to the kitchen counter and picked the sheet of paper up. Across its top in bold capital letters were the words WESTERN UNION. It was sent from Washington D.C. and addressed to Mr. and Mrs. Clarence R. Stephenson. As Ruth read its brief message, her jaw dropped. Her face took on a look of disbelief. Disbelief quickly turned to shock and a dreadful grief. Her brother had been killed.

Ruth heard weeping from the parlor. Her mother was sitting on her old, wooden rocking chair. Her head was bowed. On her lap was the children's Bible that Raymond read and studied as a boy in church school. Merle, in a voice barely audible above her whimpering, was reciting a passage from the Book of Revelation:

> *He will wipe away every tear from the eyes,*
> *and death shall be no more, neither shall there be*
> *mourning, nor crying, nor pain anymore, for the*
> *former things have passed away.*

Ruth ran upstairs to her second floor bedroom, threw herself onto her bed, buried her head in a pillow and sobbed. She loved her big brother Raymond so dearly. She looked up to him. He was like a hero to her. She cried for hours that day and for days and weeks after that.

About one hundred miles northwest of Ironton, Raymond's other sister, Marjorie, was sitting at her desk working as an administrative staff member and stenographer at Wright Army Airfield in Dayton. Marjorie received a letter from Raymond just a few weeks earlier at the end of August. She had written to Raymond asking him where the family should send his Christmas presents. In Raymond's response to Marjorie, he wrote:

> *Let everyone in the family know that they*
> *can put my presents right under the Christmas*
> *tree, because I will definitely be home by then.*

He also wrote that he had given a lot of thought about how he could provide a good home and a better life for Helen and Ann Marie after the war. He planned to become a private pilot and fly to exotic places like South America and China, working for one of the big airline companies, like TWA or Pan Am.

Marjorie had some suspicion that something may have happened to Raymond. In a letter she sent to her mother on September 25, 1944, she wrote:

> *Dear Mom,*
>
> *I kept putting off writing because I hoped to have a letter from Raymond before I wrote. Apparently he last wrote to us about the same time. In fact, I believe he mentioned in his last letter that he had written to you and Helen. He was going on a mission that night... I'm afraid something's happened.*

Marjorie was having a typical day at work until a telephone call came from her father on the same day he received the fateful telegram. He broke the news to her. In spite of her earlier suspicions, she refused to accept that Raymond was dead.

"I don't believe it, Dad. Mistakes are made all the time. I see it here at work. It has to be a mistake."

No sister and brother were closer than Marjorie and Raymond. Two years in age separated them, but they were only a grade apart in school. They were childhood playmates and as they grew, became ever closer. There were no secrets between them and they forged a bond that could never be broken.

Working at Wright Field, Marjorie knew of instances of misinformation regarding the death or capture of American soldiers. She held on to hope for months that her brother might still be alive. But, she finally succumbed to the truth in a letter she wrote to her mother on November 23, 1944:

Dear Mom,

I'm afraid it's fairly impossible for Raymond to be alive, because his plane crashed in England, so that he'd be in friendly territory. In enemy territory or some deserted place somewhere, he'd be taken prisoner and there could be a chance there was a slip up. But when the telegram said definitely that he was killed in action over England, they'd surely make sure they were right.

Raymond's mother and father were devastated. Merle lost her only son and Clarence not only lost his son, but his scouting and camping companion, fishing partner and confidant. Raymond was devoted to his parents. His father was his role model and childhood hero. Among Raymond's aspirations as a young man was to grow up to be like his dad someday. For the next few days, the Stephenson family gathered at their Ironton home with Raymond's aunts, uncles, and cousins to console one another. Six hundred miles to the east in New York City, a nineteen-year-old wife and mother had an unexpected visitor.

1880's • 1890's • 1900's • 1910's • 1920's • 1930's • 1940's • 1950's
                                                          ↑
                                                    1944-1948

A Knock at the Door

*To live in the hearts
we leave behind,
is not to die.*

— *Washington Irving*

Thump, thump, thump. There was someone at the door of the apartment on a late September afternoon. Helen placed her two-month-old daughter in her cradle before going to the door. She opened the door and was greeted by a young man.

"Hello. I have a telegram here for Mrs. Helen Stephenson."

Helen sensed from the young man's somber demeanor that something was wrong.

"I'm Helen Stephenson."

"Ma'am, I have a telegram for you. Would you please sign here?"

The delivery boy handed her a pen and clipboard. Helen's hand trembled so badly, her signature was illegible. The young man handed Helen the telegram, bid her goodbye, turned abruptly, and darted down the stairs. Helen walked back toward Ann Marie's cradle and stood by it. She stared at the envelope.

Helen believed that regardless of all of the hardships she and her family had been through as she grew up, if she kept faith and good thoughts as her mother had always encouraged her to do, all of the good things a young girl dreamed about, a loving husband, happy and healthy children, and a safe home would be hers someday. Someday arrived a year earlier when she married a young man from Ironton, Ohio of all places. Surely, God could not allow that which she loved and cherished most to be taken away from her.

Helen shook all over as she opened the envelope. The Western Union Telegram was painfully blunt and gravely to the point.

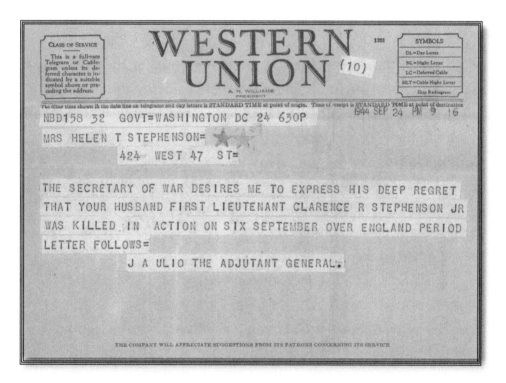

Helen was numb. The blood drained from her face. She stared at the telegram again and at the date, SIX SEPTEMBER. Their first wedding anniversary and her nineteenth birthday. It was a day that she celebrated quietly with her mother and her baby daughter little more than two weeks earlier. How cruel. She read the telegram a third time. The message sunk in. Her legs wobbled beneath her. Helen's throat tightened as her lungs gasped for air. She painfully cried out.

"My Raymond is gone!" And the sobbing commenced.

She picked Ann Marie up out of the cradle and clutched her daughter in her arms. She could hardly breathe through her gasps and tears. When she read those words, her heart broke, and a piece of her died inside that day along with Raymond.

Her mother heard Helen's cries and Maggie came running into the bedroom. Without a word being said, as soon as Maggie saw her daughter with a telegram in her hand, she knew. Up and down 47th Street, Maggie saw all too many Gold Stars hung in tenement room windows symbolizing the home of a fallen soldier, not to know. With four of her own sons in the army along with her son-in-law Raymond, the thought crossed her mind every day that she might be the next resident of 47th Street to hang a gold star on the front window of her apartment.

"Why?" Helen questioned her mother, as she fought through her tears and anguish to speak. "Why did this happen to Raymond? We had so many dreams for our lives after the war. Raymond's never even seen his daughter and she'll never see her father."

There was nothing that Maggie Gregg could say to Helen to alleviate her pain and grief. She didn't even try. She wrapped her arms around Helen with Ann Marie still cradled in her daughter's arms. She prayed silently for Raymond's soul. She asked God that in time, He might grant Helen peace of mind and a mended heart. Helen spent some time that day and each day for months thereafter sitting in a pew at Sacred Heart Church, praying for Raymond and searching for consolation.

Helen took some solace in that she sent the photograph of Ann Marie and her taken with that old, pawn shop bought camera to Raymond. At least he saw a picture of his beautiful daughter before he perished. But, even that bit of consolation was dashed, when the envelope that contained the letter and photograph that Helen had sent to her husband in England was returned unopened. It had arrived at the Watton Royal Air Force base just after his death.

Peace of mind for Helen was elusive. Other than the fact that Raymond was dead, she didn't know anything about how it happened. She had no idea what was done with his remains, or even if there were remains recovered to bury. There was no closure for her.

For many months Helen shed thousands of tears for Raymond. There were many sleepless nights and others that brought nightmares, as Helen's imagination conjured up images of how Raymond might have perished. Was he shot? Did he crash? Was his base attacked? Did he die quickly? Did he suffer? Dozens of questions flashed through her mind, all with no answer. Painful images tormented her. Helen constantly carried an enormous weight. If she didn't have Ann Marie to care for, she wouldn't have gotten out of bed most days.

About the time of the first anniversary of Raymond's death, Helen was still in the dark regarding how he died and where he was buried. She wrote to the War Department in September 1945 looking for whatever information she could glean about her late husband and specifically, asked for a photograph of his final resting place. Helen exchanged letters with Raymond's sister Marjorie, but she knew nothing more than Helen. With so much time having passed with nothing more than a telegram to go by, Helen had begun to hope that the notification of Raymond's death may have been sent in error. It wouldn't have been the first time that a mistake was made. She knelt by the side of her bed every night before going to sleep, praying for a miracle. The Bible was full of miracles. Why shouldn't there be one for her?

On October 6, 1945, the Quartermaster General's Office responded to Helen. There was no miracle. The army confirmed that Raymond had been killed and was interred at the United States Military Cemetery in England, about forty-two miles northeast of London, near Cambridge. The letter noted the location of his grave (Plot Q, Row 3, Grave 14). The Quartermaster General also wrote that there were no provisions under which a photograph of his grave could be taken and sent to her.

Another year went by. An undeterred Helen Stephenson inquired again in the fall of 1946 about her late husband. Another letter from the Quartermaster General was issued on February 3, 1947 informing Helen that the United States Military Cemetery near Cambridge was a *temporary resting place* until Raymond's remains and those of thousands of other soldiers, sailors, and Marines could be placed in a permanent American cemetery overseas, or returned home for a final burial in accordance with the wishes of the next of kin. The letter also indicated that *the evacuation of the remains of Lieutenant Stephenson would be in progress by October 1947*, a bit more than three years after his fatal crash. Helen again did not receive a photograph of Raymond's grave as she had requested. Rather, she was sent an aerial photograph of the entire cemetery where he was laid to rest.

Helen continued to live with her mother on 47th Street. She took a part-time job at a Coty cosmetics and perfume facility packing boxes. Maggie watched Ann Marie while Helen was at work. Her job was one of the few distractions she had from thinking about how much she missed Raymond.

Helen exchanged additional correspondence with the Office of the Quartermaster General. October 1947 came and went without the return of her husband's body to her. It was another nine months later during July of 1948, that Raymond's

remains were exhumed in England. His body was flown to New York City and then transported by train back to his hometown of Ironton. Helen figured that Raymond would have wanted that. He loved the little city in which he was raised. He could have been buried at Arlington National Cemetery, but Helen wanted his family to be able to visit his final resting place. Helen followed Raymond's remains out to Ohio for his funeral and burial, accompanied on the train by Ann Marie and Helen's brother, Willie.

At two o'clock in the afternoon on July 25, 1948, Helen, Ann Marie, who had just turned four years old, and Willie attended a solemn funeral service at the Phillips Funeral Home in Ironton, along with Raymond's parents, sisters, and other close family and friends. Raymond's casket was draped with an American flag at the head of the room. It was flanked by large arrangements of flowers of every color and variety. A photograph of

1st Lt. C. R.
STEPHENSON, Jr.

Born
NOVEMBER 8, 1920

Died
SEPTEMBER 6, 1944

Services at
PHILLIPS FUNERAL HOME
SUNDAY, JULY 25, 1948
2:00 P. M.

Clergyman
REV. CLARENCE CORN

Burial
WOODLAND CEMETERY

Raymond in uniform as an air corps cadet was displayed on top of the coffin. Helen was heartbroken all over again reliving the pain of the loss of the only man she ever loved. Even though it was emotionally agonizing, she was grateful that after waiting nearly four years, she finally had a chance to tell her Raymond goodbye.

Ann Marie saw that everyone was sad that day, but no one told her why.

"Mommy, why is everyone so sad?"

"It's just a sad day, Ann Marie."

"Who is the man in the picture on the box?"

"It's just someone we know honey."

Being only four years old, everyone wanted to protect her from the truth and the hurt.

Following the funeral service that was conducted by the Reverend Clarence Corn of the Ironton First Baptist Church, Raymond's flag covered casket was escorted from the funeral home to a hearse waiting outside. The party of grieving family and friends followed the hearse carrying Raymond for the short drive to Woodland Cemetery, also known as Ironton's City of the Dead. Raymond's final resting place was among other deceased members of the United States armed forces dating as far back as the Civil War.

Ann Marie, age 4, in Ironton, Ohio for her father's funeral.

The hearse drove through the gated cemetery entrance with its impressive stone arch, engraved with the name of the cemetery. The cemetery had perfectly manicured lawns. Its paths were lined with a canopy of mature oaks and elms. Along a gentle slope near the southern edge of the cemetery, were hundreds of small red, white, and blue flags, one gracing each stone bearing the name of a soldier, sailor, or Marine lost in the service of his country.

Woodland Cemetery, also known as Ironton's, City of the Dead.

A tent had been erected over Raymond's grave to protect him and the grieving family and friends who came to bid him farewell from the light rain that fell that day. The pinging sound of the raindrops against the tent's canvas roof provided a background of naturally soothing sound as the minister prayed aloud for the repose of Raymond's soul. His mom, dad, and sisters, held hands and wept alongside Helen as the prayers were recited. As a final salute to this brave fallen aviator, the military honor guard crisply folded the American flag that had adorned Raymond's dark, wooden casket. After the last of thirteen folds were made to the flag, a soldier approached Helen and handed it to her.

"Mrs. Stephenson, this flag is presented on behalf of a grateful nation as a symbol for your loved one's honorable and faithful service."

The bugler played taps as Helen embraced the flag against her chest with one hand, while holding little Ann Marie's hand with the other. If there was ever a test as to whether God really does only give crosses to those that can bear them, this was Helen's.

The Letter

More than kisses, letters mingle souls.
— *John Donne*

Mom and I sat there on her bed while the rest of the family chatted and ate birthday cake in the dining room. It was heart breaking for me to watch my eighty-year-old mom cry. During my fifty years, I remembered seeing her cry on only two other occasions. The first was when her brother Joey died of lung cancer at the age of thirty nine. The other, was when her mother passed away.

My hand trembled as I held the antiquated piece of note paper on which Raymond had so carefully and lovingly penned his final sentiments to his wife, my mother. I tried to continue reading the letter to Mom and my voice cracked. As I held her hand, it was as though she shared her emotions with me. I could feel her pain in my own heart.

"Raymond," Mom interrupted. "Would you please start again from the very beginning?"

"Of course, Mom."

"The 5th of September, 1944." It was the day before Raymond died.

Tuesday, 12:15 P.M. 5 Sept. '44

My Dearest Darling,

    I am sitting in the lounge of the
Officers Club after just finishing a dinner
of baked ham, potatoes, soup, and apple pie.
I decided to bring my writing tablet to
dinner with me, since I have until one
o'clock before I go on duty, and I have been
having trouble lately finding time to write
letters. But I'm sure you will forgive
me, because I am working harder so I can
get home sooner and be with my most
beloved wife and daughter. Joe and some
others of my crew are flying missions
about every other day so they can catch
up with me. I'm farther ahead in time
than the rest of the crew, having only

three missions to go. I am a Flight
Commander now, and I can schedule my
crew to fly anytime I want to, and I am
losing no time in doing it. I received two
letters from you, one written August 24,
and the other Aug. 27. Taking out an insurance
policy for Ann was a very good idea. I'm
glad you did. I'm sure crazy to see you
and Ann both. Of course she is bound to be
beautiful if she looks anything like me. Ahem!
Well, I haven't much else to write about,
so I'll close for now. I love you and
miss you very. very. very much, sweetheart

All My Love,

Ray

After I finished reading the letter aloud, Mom and I sat on the edge of the bed, both of us with tears on our cheeks.

"Why did you wait so long to show this to me, Mom? Why didn't you ever tell me anything about your first husband?"

Maybe she thought I'd consider it disloyal to her second husband, my father. "Why talk about it now and why only with me?"

While she blotted away tears from her eyes, she answered.

"When I was pregnant with you, your father and me were thinking and talking about girls and boys names. Your older brother, being the first son, was obviously named Joseph after your father. I suggested the name Raymond if I had a boy. Your father told me he thought it would be nice to name him after his Uncle Ray."

Mom paused for a minute and leaned a bit closer, softening her voice.

"I never really gave a second's worth of thought about naming you after his Uncle Ray. To appease your father and not hurt his feelings, I just agreed with him and said, sure. Your father loved the idea. The truth is, I wanted to call you Raymond just like I called my first husband Raymond. I named you after him."

There I was, fifty- ears-old and discovering I was the namesake of a brave young B-17 pilot who lost his life in World War II. My mother's first love. Mom hesitated telling me or anyone else in the family about who my namesake really was, because she did not want to hurt my father's feelings. Mom loved my father very much. He was a good man, a hard worker, and a good provider who loved his family.

"Raymond, do you think it's possible to love two people at the same time? And if you did, would it be wrong? God forgive me if it is."

There was a loaded question. I didn't know how to answer it, so I thought it best to answer her question with one of my own.

"Well, what do you think, Mom?"

"You know I love your father very much," Mom responded unhesitatingly. "But, I never stopped loving Raymond. I kept that letter in that box and near my bed all these years. I can't help but think of the day Raymond and I met and how we fell in love. My eighteenth birthday when we got married was the happiest day of my life. When Raymond was killed on our first anniversary and my nineteenth birthday, September 6th became a day I never wanted to celebrate again. It became the saddest day of my life back in 1944 and a day to regret ever since. The only thing that gives me some comfort is reading this beautiful letter that my Raymond wrote the day before he was taken from me. I pull it out of that old wooden box every year on my birthday, read it, and say a prayer for Raymond."

Who knows what would have happened over time to Mom and Raymond had he not died in the fiery crash that claimed his life and the lives of most of his crew? Mom never got to see him grow old or frail. They never argued over how to raise the kids or how to manage the household budget. Could they have held onto the magic that was their instantaneous, deep, and abiding love for each other? Who knows? However, sixty one years after his death, in her mind and in her heart, she still only saw the dashing, confident, and romantic young aviator that swept her off her feet in New York's Central Park on a beautiful summer afternoon in 1942.

"Yes, Mom," I finally answered her. "It is possible to love more than one person at a time and to love them in different ways. And you don't need to ask forgiveness of God or anyone else for feeling that way. I think each of us carries in our hearts one special love for our lifetime. If we're lucky, we get to spend our entire life with that extraordinary love. Sometimes they're with us for only a short time. Just because you fell in love again, doesn't mean that the special place in your heart for Raymond need be any less devoted to your memories of him."

Mom smiled. We sat on the bed a bit longer as she gently began to put Raymond's last letter back in its envelope and return it to the wooden box where it resided for six decades. She placed the box back into the bottom drawer of her dresser and then turned toward me with a puzzled expression on her face.

"Why me?" Mom now asked.

"I'm not sure what you're asking me, Mom."

"Why do you suppose I am the last one to go? My Raymond, my mother and Pop, all five of my brothers and both of my sisters. Why did God decide he would take me last? Saying goodbye and letting them go was so hard." The tears flowed again.

"The last time I saw my father was about four years after Raymond died. He was committed to Central Islip State Hospital. Me and my brother Marty took the train out there once after Pop had been gone a few months. When we saw him he didn't even recognize us. It was terrible. People were screaming. Patient's clothes were dirty and there was a smell of urine. Pop was in a strait jacket mumbling to himself. He died in that awful place shortly after you were born. He was really a gentle soul and didn't deserve to die like that."

Joey dying at just thirty-nine broke Mom's heart. Peter was still a young man when mysteriously, he was found dead at JFK Airport. The rest of her brothers, sisters, and her mother lasted to older ages, but it still wasn't easy when they left her.

Mom and her mother Maggie, during difficult times, often said that God only gives crosses to those who can bear them. My mother often told me about her own mother's strength and patience. She bore more than her share of crosses during her lifetime. Like Mom, Maggie Gregg was the last of her own generation to pass.

"Mom, the way I see it, God needed you to stay on this earth longer than the rest of them, because you were the strongest. He knew that you would care for them and those close to them in their times of sickness, weakness, and when each of them was called to Heaven. He knew that you had the same strength, patience, and the grace that your mother had. He was right. You loved them all so much and took such good care of all of them, just like you've always loved and taken such good care of me."

Mom patted my hand. A grin replaced her frown.

"There was another important reason why you're still here Mom. I think God had one more important task He needed you to accomplish before you're called to Heaven. He couldn't let you leave me until you were ready to tell me this story."

"It's strange, Raymond. I can't always remember what I had for breakfast, but I relive the smallest details of my time with Raymond. All the joy and all the sadness. The war was so terrible. It killed the sons, husbands, fathers, and brothers of so many people and killed so many dreams too."

Mom never had a lot of big dreams growing up. She was so poor and forever struggling. She figured that was her station in life.

"But, then my Raymond came to me. There was love and hope and a dream of a happy life together. When the war killed Raymond, it killed most of my dreams for us too. Our married life together lasted exactly one year. It was the best year of our lives. After the crash, I didn't want to believe Raymond was really dead and it wasn't until we buried him in Ironton four years after he died, that I finally came to grips with it. I was so badly bruised so young in life, but thank God I never broke, because there was one dream of ours I had to fulfill and a promise I had to keep."

"Tell me about the dream, Mom."

"Well, Raymond, I have one more story to tell you."

Mom reminded me about the time she and my father came to visit me and my wife Mary when we lived in San Diego. My mother had never been on an airplane before and was terrified to fly. It stunned me when she called to say that she and my dad wanted to fly from New York to California to see us. Equally surprising was after their arrival in San Diego, my mother wanted me to bring her to the beach one day during her stay. My dad always took my brothers, sister, and me to Coney Island in Brooklyn or Jones Beach on Long Island when we were kids. Mom never had an interest in going to the beach, especially since she didn't know how to swim.

"I had two reasons for coming to California," Mom explained. "Of course, I wanted to see you and Mary, but I had some unfinished business to take care of. My Raymond and I made a promise to each other the summer when we first met in 1942. We were standing in the Atlantic Ocean together at Coney Island. I was only sixteen years old. Raymond told me that when he was a boy, he dreamed of traveling from Ohio to both the east and the west coasts to go in the world's two biggest oceans. That day at Coney Island we satisfied half of that dream together. We promised that we would go to the west coast some day and go in the Pacific Ocean for the first time together. I needed to keep that promise and fulfill that dream for the two of us. If I didn't come out to California and have you take me to the beach, I don't think I ever would have done it."

It seemed insignificant to me at the time, but Mom, my father, my wife Mary and I went to Coronado Island one day. Mom asked me to walk across Coronado's beach of golden sand with her. When we reached the water's edge, we slipped off our shoes. Mom took my hand. We walked a few steps westward and placed our feet in the cool blue waters of the Pacific Ocean. Both of us looked out over the sea as the sun glistened off the water. We listened as the gentle waves caressed the shore.

"On that day in California, I finally kept the promise I made at Coney Island during the summer that Raymond and I fell in love."

Mom's eyes swelled with tears again and she squeezed my hand. She looked into my eyes with an earnestness that warmed my heart.

"There are some dreams that you can't let die and some promises that should never be broken. It took me a very long time, but I finally did stand in the Pacific Ocean… and I even did it with my Raymond, just like I promised."

Raymond's final resting place, Woodland Cemetery, Ironton, Ohio.

Epilogue

"... let us strive to finish the work we are in,
to bind up the nation's wounds,
to care for him who shall have borne the battle
and for his widow and orphan...
— *Abraham Lincoln*

The reminders of the war were everywhere for Helen. Gold stars hung on the front doors and in the windows of the homes and apartments of mothers and wives who lost their sons or husbands. A young neighborhood friend could be recognized from across the street or down the block, not because of the sight of his face or the sound of his voice, but by the clicking of metal hooks that extended from his sleeves where his hands were before he lost them in the war. The infirmed, the disfigured and the disabled weren't hard to find. Almost three hundred thousand soldiers, sailors and aviators were killed in the war. Another six hundred and seventy thousand were wounded.

World War II brought Raymond and Helen together. Ironically, it was the war that tore them apart. As short as their life together was, and as devastating as Raymond's death was to her, Helen never regretted that brief, extraordinary time with one another.

Many relationships were shrouded in mystery during the war. Raymond's co-pilot, Joe Ward, who married his young bride Kay shortly before their crew shipped out from Louisiana to their duty station in England, told almost no one about his marriage. After the crew departed, Kay returned to her family's home in Arkansas. When she stopped receiving letters from Joe in the fall of 1944, she wrote a letter to his parents in New Jersey asking if they had heard from him. The arrival of her letter came as a shock to the Wards, as Joe never told his parents he was married.

Joe Minery, one of the survivors of the September 6, 1944 B-17 crash, returned to his hometown in Connecticut after the war. Joe married and settled in Meriden, Connecticut. He had a successful career in the insurance business.

Keith Clinton was the sole living member of the B-17 crew when I made his acquaintance on March 31, 2012. After searching for contact information, I called him on the telephone.

"Hi. Is this Mr. Keith Clinton?"

"Yes, it is. Who's calling?"

"Mr. Clinton, my name is Ray O'Conor. We've never met or spoken before and you don't know me. But, my mother is the widow of your B-17 pilot, Clarence Raymond Stephenson."

"No kidding? How is Helen?"

"Mom is just fine, sir. How are you?"

"Not bad, all things considered and still above ground."

"Mr. Clinton, I don't want to be a pest, but I'm working on a project. Do you think if I come out to your home in Michigan, that you might have some time to speak with me about Raymond, the crew and your experiences during the war?"

"Well, what are you doing next Saturday?"

"I think I'm getting on a plane for Michigan, Mr. Clinton."

Mr. Clinton and I were joined by his wife Evelyn, whom he met at Chanute Field in Illinois after he returned from his service in Europe. Mrs. Clinton was a member of the Women's Army Corps. The Clinton's daughters, Loraine and Adele, were also at the Clinton's home when we met. We sat around their kitchen table for hours as Mr. Clinton shared stories, as well as dozens of documents and photographs from the time of his service with his crew in England. Mr. Clinton worked in the construction industry for many years. He performed missionary work through his church for those less fortunate.

Raymond Stephenson's family suffered the devastating loss of a son and brother.   No family ever raised a finer son. I visited his sisters Marjorie and Ruth in February 2013, ages ninety and eighty-three respectively at the time. They cried when they told me the stories of how they learned of their brother's death. It was almost seventy years since that fateful day. Both still have a special place in their heart for their big brother. They said their mother and father were never the same after the war and Raymond's death.

Marjorie Stephenson Miller, the older of Raymond's kid sisters, spent her entire life in Ohio. She and her husband, Elbert Miller, had four children. The first, a son named Tommy, passed away at the age of two. Two more sons and a daughter blessed the Miller family. Tragedy struck again though, when cancer claimed the life of her daughter Barbara at the age of fifty-five. As Marjorie told me the stories of her family and the losses she suffered beginning with Raymond, her sorrow was evident, but there wasn't a trace of bitterness. Marjorie passed away in 2014 at the age of ninety-one. She asked me to tell folks who read this book that, "Raymond was a great big brother."

Ruth Stephenson Hughes, Raymond's youngest sister, also remained in Ohio where she still resides. She married

Robert Hughes, a Baptist minister, and was a constant source of support for her husband and his congregation. She raised eight children. She too, lost a daughter, Debbie, who was killed in a highway traffic accident at age fifty-one. When I sat with Ruth in her Ohio home, along with her husband and oldest daughter Stephanie, she shared wonderful stories and showed me pictures of her children, grandchildren and great-grandchildren, of whom she could not be more proud. She gave me an unexpected and priceless gift, Raymond's diary. Neither his widow Helen, nor daughter Ann Marie, knew he kept one.

I called my mother and sister from my hotel room in Ohio after receiving Raymond's diary. I read passages to them over the telephone written the day Mom and Raymond first met, after their first date, and when they parted company. The diary brought great joy and comfort to Mom and Ann Marie.

Raymond's best friend and cousin, Jack Bradshaw, managed to come home safely after World War II. He passed away in Ohio at the age of ninety-two in 2012.

Helen's mother Maggie could have had an easier life had she parted company with Pop. A priest told her she could have had her marriage annulled, because Pop's mental illness wasn't disclosed to her before they got married. Maggie believed in the caption of her wedding vows that read for better or worse. She wouldn't leave Pop and the four young children from his first marriage. She had a heavy cross to bear, but what she preached, she also abided by, convinced that God only gives crosses to those that can bear them.

Maggie spent most of her remaining life in New York City. She became a United States citizen in 1937. No one was more pleased to become an American or prouder of the military service her sons and son-in-law rendered to her adopted country. She lived to the age of eighty-nine.

Helen's brother Marty devoted his post-war life to home schooling physically challenged children in many of New York City's poorest and roughest neighborhoods. He was robbed with such frequency that he purchased a supply of cheap watches and inexpensive wallets, placing five dollars in each one. Every Christmas he anonymously sent a toy or clothing to each of his students in the mail. The return address printed on each of the parcels stated only Santa Claus – North Pole. Marty passed away at the age of ninety-four.

Although physically whole after the war, Helen's brother Willie suffered from a broken heart. When he arrived home in New York City, Willie stopped by the apartment of his girlfriend to ask the girl he loved to marry him. Her parents told him that she had a calling and left home to join a convent in Montreal. Willie took a train to Montreal hoping he could convince her that she belonged with him. He wouldn't get the chance. He was denied permission to enter the convent grounds or speak with his former girlfriend.

Helen was closest of all to her brother Joey. Although a kind, intelligent, fit, and handsome gentleman, he never married. He was a happy bachelor and enjoyed a large cadre of friends and all that New York City had to offer. He was a deeply loving and caring man. He endeared himself to everyone who knew him.

I recall as a teenager the day the call came to our house from Joey's doctor telling Mom that he had succumbed to lung cancer at the age of thirty-nine. I don't remember her ever crying when I was a kid. She was always so steady and strong. Moments after she lifted the phone to her ear, the sobbing started. If her reaction to Joey's death was any indication of the depth of the love that Mom had for Raymond, the telegram notifying her that he had died in the war must have nearly killed her.

In 2010, Mom was unable to live independently and Ann Marie invited her to move into her Long Island home. Ann Marie was widowed several years earlier when her husband Carl passed away unexpectedly from a stroke. She has a son, daughter and four grandchildren who live nearby. Like our mother and

Ann Marie, age 5 and Helen in New York City, 1950.

grandmother before her, Ann Marie is loving, compassionate, and made of tough stuff. She had an earlier marriage to an alcoholic and despite her efforts to help him, was left with no alternative but to dissolve the marriage. Life as a single mom was a cross that she bore for many years, but she did have the support of our mother, who helped care for Ann Marie's son and daughter while she worked as a probation officer. Ann Marie is a breast cancer survivor.

My father, Helen's second husband Joseph O'Conor, passed away in 2010 at the age of eighty-six. He was a combat veteran of the Korean War and a successful attorney.

This story ends pretty much where it started, with me driving from Saratoga Springs to Long Island to see Mom one final time. As I rolled along the highway, I wondered if everyone lives two lives… the one you really live and the one you let other people see. History can't be unlived, but it can be buried from our consciousness. For more than sixty years, Mom left some secrets and stories in the past. Well, at least until she reached her eightieth birthday.

She passed away on November 4, 2013, surrounded by family and loved ones. Her last few months were spent at Saint Joseph's Home for the Aged in Huntington, New York, under the care of an extraordinary group of women, the Missionary Sisters of Saint Benedict.

In her room were a few items that held a special place in Mom's heart. On the nightstand she had a small photo album with pictures of her children, grandchildren and great-grandchildren. Her rosary beads dangled from the bed post and a crucifix from the Holy Land adorned the wall across from her bed. Her room looked out onto a lush garden of greens and flowers of every natural color in God's creation. In its center was a grotto devoted to The Blessed Mother. A gentle waterfall flowed through it. Viewing it through her bedroom window brought a heavenly peace to her. Mom's deep faith was the foundation of her strength and character. It guided her through troubled waters for eighty-eight years.

Sister Pia Wojtak, who was very fond of Mom, went to her room at St. Joseph's in the wee hours of the morning she died. Mom was unconscious and her time drawing near. Sister Pia told Mom that she had to travel to Maryland that day and if Mom passed while she was away, to send her a sign to let her know.

Sister Pia and the other Sisters with whom she was traveling, stopped for a cup of coffee along the New Jersey Turnpike on the way to Maryland at 9:30 a.m. When they returned to their car it wouldn't start. The battery was dead. A gentleman jump started their car and they got back on the road. Shortly thereafter, Sr. Pia received a call on her cell phone from Saint Joseph's. Helen had passed away. Sister Pia asked when she died. 9:30 a.m. The rest of the trip to and from Maryland was uneventful. The car started with no problems. The battery was fine.

Mom was buried at Calverton National Cemetery with her second husband, my father, with whom she had been happily married for fifty-seven years. She brought a piece of Raymond with her though. Almost seventy years earlier, Raymond gave her a beautiful silver locket before he went off to war. In it is a picture of the two of them and an inscription…Love Always. Helen cherished it. Ann Marie pinned it to her blouse before she was laid to rest.

God be with you. God bless you. God save you, Mom.

Acknowledgments

I came home from the office one day and told my wife I wanted to quit my job to work on this project.

"Mary, I'm going to leave the bank to work on the book full time."

"Are you having a midlife crisis?"

"I don't think so."

"Well, whatever you decide to do, I'm with you one hundred percent."

Thank you Mary, for your support and love. I could have never done this without you. I love you.

My son Brian's guidance and editing work were more helpful than he knows. He is an exceptional writer. My daughter Meghan lifts my mood with her positive attitude and loving spirit. My grandson Jack's smile, innocence, playfulness and hugs got Bwabwa through many rough days. I love you guys.

My sister Ann Marie was not only a valuable resource for photographs, letters and other documents, but entertained my constant phone calls and questions. She gave me insights into the lives of our mother, grandmother and family, that no one else could. I see all of the outstanding qualities of Mom and our grandmother in her. I love you, Annie.

I would be remiss if I didn't acknowledge my brothers, Joe and Marty. We shared a bedroom and bunk beds growing up. We played together often. We fought and got into trouble occasionally. But, we always loved one another and a guy couldn't have had better brothers.

The first person outside my family whose advice I sought when I started this project was Winnie Yu, an exceptional writer and an even better person. Thank you, Winnie, for your advice and encouragement.

Teri Gay's pearls of wisdom, willingness to help and her unbridled enthusiasm were great motivators for me. You are a good friend.

My friend and entrepreneur, Nancy Holzman, believed in my ability to write this story so strongly, that she helped me believe it myself. *Whatever you can do or dream you can, begin it. Boldness has genius, power and magic in it. (Goethe)*

Best-selling author James Bradley (*Flags of Our Fathers, Fly Boys*) didn't know me when I contacted him out of the blue a few years ago. His willingness to share his time, experience and wisdom with me is of incalculable value.

I met reporter Shane Arrington and Executive Editor Mike Caldwell of The Tribune in Ironton on a research trip to Ohio. The newspaper not only opened their records to me, but Shane wrote and Mike published a superb feature article about my journey to tell the story of my namesake and the woman he loved. The article helped uncover important sources of information. Thank you, gentlemen.

I called the Briggs Library in Ironton and made an appointment to meet with Mary Counts of the library's genealogy room. When I arrived for our meeting, a woman in the genealogy room, Marta Ramey, told me Mary no longer worked there and had left the area. After noticing a dejected look on my face, Marta asked, "Are you the guy writing the book about the B-17 pilot from Ironton?" "Yes, I am." Marta pulled a large envelope from her desk. "Mary said you were coming. She did a lot of research on the Stephenson family, copied newspaper articles, and found some other items that may help you." Since then, Marta has also been very helpful providing information and photographs. Thank you Mary and Marta. The Briggs Library is a wonderful community resource.

A number of trusted friends served as beta readers. Thank you Joanne Martin, Bob Campchero, Scott McLoud, Matt Dill, Lori Munn, Winnie Yu, Teri Gay, Manny Cirenza, Joe Murphy, Linda and Bill Gibeault, and Denise Romand. Your feedback was of great value.

I learned more about writing at my first session at The New York State Summer Writers Institute, hosted by Skidmore College, than I had in a lifetime. Adam Braver, Danzy Senna and other superb writers, including my session colleagues, generously shared their knowledge and experience. It made me a much better writer. I owe a special debt of gratitude to Amy Wallen, whose review and critique of my manuscript and sound advice were especially valuable.

Mr. Keith Clinton, his wife Evelyn, and daughters Adele and Lorraine allowed a stranger in pursuit of a story into their home and lives. Mr. Clinton shared his experiences, memories, records and photographs, for which I am so grateful. He exemplifies the best of America's Greatest Generation.

Thank you Marjorie Stephenson Miller and Ruth Stephenson Hughes. These gracious women shared a very painful part of their lives with me. Mrs. Miller and her family, Randy, Jackie and Mick Miller and John Jewell, made me feel like family when I visited them in their Ohio home. Photographs and letters were among the priceless items I received from them. Mrs. Hughes, her husband Robert and their oldest daughter, Stephanie House Colton, not only entrusted me with Raymond's diary, but Stephanie and her husband Steve met me in New York months after my Ohio visit and brought more than one hundred family letters dating back more than seventy years. Making the acquaintance and forging a relationship with these families is a gift. My sincere thanks to all of you.

Debbi Wraga at ShiresPress is exceptional at her craft. She, her company and its related Northshire Bookstores, remind us of the importance of writing, reading and responsible publishing.

My father taught me about hard work and its rewards. He helped raise four children while working and going to law school full time. He gave me an opportunity for an education and a prosperous life. He was a great guy. I love you, Pop.

Finally, thank you, Mom, for entrusting this story to me. I hope I didn't let you down. I miss you and love you.

Your Raymond

Helen and her son, Raymond, 2011.

About The Author

Ray O'Conor has been a weekly newspaper columnist and author of articles and opinion pieces published in several newspapers and magazines. His work as an author of narrative non-fiction has been the subject of stories and articles across broadcast, print and digital media.

Ray left his position as a bank CEO and senior officer of a publicly traded company to pursue his writing career. He also served as a Special Agent with the United States Department of Defense.

Ray has a lifetime of involvement with many charitable causes and community based organizations. Among other recognitions, he was named a General Mills' "Wheaties Everyday Champion", is the recipient of the Distinguished Leadership Award by the National Association for Community Leadership, the American Bar Association's Liberty Bell Award, the Centennial Good Scout Award from the Boy Scouts of America and the U.S. Department of Health and Human Services' National Community Action Award.

His avocation is participating in endurance sports and mountain climbing.

CPSIA information can be obtained
at www.ICGtesting.com
Printed in the USA
BVOW07s2303300616
454016BV00004B/5/P